Frena Gray-Davidson

Speaking Dementia

# SPEAKING DEMENTIA
## Revised Edition

## FRENA GRAY-DAVIDSON

Balian Books
2012 Bisbee,
Arizona

ISBN 9780615536583 Dementia/ Caregiving/Communication

Cover Design: department
Cover and Author Photographs: Lizann Michaud

# Table of Contents

## SECTION THREE: GROWING YOUR CAREGIVER HEART

## SECTION FOUR: THE SUNDOWNING SECTION

## Author's Introduction

This is my fifth book on dementia and here I've totally revised the way I share the information that comes from my 20-plus years caregiving people with dementia and facilitating support groups.

My other books were put together in the rational step-by-step way that how-to books are usually done. Because editors made me do that and, as a professional writer, I thought that was how to do it too. And, plus, I'm a slow learner.

I wasn't paying real attention to something I knew perfectly well. It's this: other people, who aren't caregivers, might be able to sit and read uninterruptedly in peace and quiet.

However, life as a caregiver is very different. How often do you get to sit down in a leisurely way and just read through a whole book when you're a caregiver? You and I know the answer to that, don't we?

And, let's face it, if you did read a whole book, you'd prefer it to be a mystery novel or something fun, wouldn't you? And I understand that perfectly.

I also wanted to address more strongly another issue that I have noticed through my work with support groups and training workshops. The most stressful thing for caregivers is when they set themselves up to fight against or deny the basic elements of dementia. To attach real urgency to re-training a person with dementia who has lost a skill. To be angry at someone's perfectly normal dementia failing, like short-term memory issues.

Of course, this is our stress at work. No blame in that. However, we would all find our caregiving day much easier if we did not pick the unwinnable battle to fight.

I've tried to ensure that you hear repetitively which battles you won't win. Because I know at some point you'll take that in and it will help you set down a great burden.

As one woman said to me in a workshop, "You mean, I don't have to try to stop my Mom's dementia?"

"That's absolutely right," I nodded.

"You mean, I could just concentrate on trying to have fun with her?"

"Heck yes!" Big affirmation from me and also other people in that workshop. "And—guess what?—your Mom wishes you would get on with the fun!"

And we all wish we could get on with the fun—and I promise you, there can be plenty of fun in the average dementia day. But first, many of us have to put aside our own rigidity and fearfulness so we can move to that other place where the fun people hang out.

So I've done this book in broad sections, broken down into niblets, nuggets and chunks, so you can sit down, pick something you need to know about and digest it immediately.

I want my information to become an immediate tool for you. You'll find I've also included nuggets, based on articles I've written, that cover the same information. This is because I find, as a dementia educator, that we caregivers are more receptive at some times than others.

My experience is that a caregiver can hear the same essential information over and over until one day—the right day—that person really hears it. Really absorbs it. Really gets it.

That's why I've chosen to do this book in a way which includes repetition of information. I considered whether to edit all that out of my original articles and decided against it.

So, if you find yourself thinking "She already said that!", then congratulations! Because you already really heard that. Move forward to the next nugget.

Besides being divided into broad sections, you will also find a title listing for every nugget in each section, so you can find your subject or your need addressed.

10

And if you find it's not there, email me, and the next edition will be better for someone else because you did. You'll find my contact information at the back of this book. And thank-you in advance.

I also want to thank you for being a dementia caregiver. Whether you care for a family member at home, whether you're a member of the care staff in a care home, facility or day program, I want to thank you.

You know, most people out there don't want to do what we do. They turn away with fear or dread and cross their fingers, hoping that'll keep dementia away.

They don't know that we walk in the great heart of life. We walk as companions and helpers with people who need us to be their mothers and fathers and, in doing our sacred work of companionship, we go right to the center of heart. Ours and theirs.

That makes what we do so very healing, for those we care for and of course most of all for ourselves. I have certainly found that to be true.

But I've also found that better understanding, being able to forgive and letting go of being rigid and controlling, have all helped me even more to enter and enjoy this great work of the spirit.

So thank-you, all my great teachers of dementia. Thank-you to my wonderful fellow workers and fellow walkers. And thank-you. Yes, you. You know who you are. You.

Thank-you most of all.

I've been a caregiver of people with dementia for over twenty years now. And I have to say, they always made sense to me. From the very first one—a 79-year-old woman diagnosed with Alzheimer's, living in Berkeley, California.

I stayed there for a year—because I really liked her, because she made sense to me, because her family seemed to make little effort to understand or empathize with her condition. They did, however, try to get care gathered around her from others and did that innovatively and well. I felt for her sense of loss and isolation from her three sons, who seemed distant or angry with her because of her illness.

To me, she seemed like someone stranded on a desert island in the middle of family struggle. At that point, I didn't know how typical all that anger, rejection and reproach was in the Alzheimer's family. I would gradually find out how rare it is for a family to come together in peace, mutual respect and love for their parent with dementia and make a working plan.

When I say that people with dementia make sense to me, that doesn't mean I always understand. I don't always grasp how exactly they make sense on every occasion. That's what keeps me interested. Because I know when I don't understand, it's not their fault. It's my lack. And, as any of my friends would tell you, I have plenty of lack. But I do know what it is to deal with family extremity and that gives me a whole sense of connection with others in that same struggling place.

12

And I admire very much the determination that people with dementia have to bring to their situation. They not only have to deal with their own struggle, but they are also subjected to the suffering of those who mourn their loss, even while they are living.

I find myself moved and, yes, fascinated by their situation. After all, how do people manage to face the struggle to communicate their own essential being? How do they deal with the struggle to be fully human when society thinks that they no longer are?

How do they live in that frightening place? How do they live so often with humor, usually without bitterness and with some innate wisdom that still connects them with life and relationship —even in the middle of family confusion, loss of all security of knowing and the unreasonable demands of others?

In many ways, our society is more compassionate and more insightful about what disability and function loss mean to other human beings than we used to be. We are learning to under-

-stand that having physical disability or being developmentally disabled does not mean being cut off from human endeavor, triumph and spirit.

However, alas, that compassion seems to be generally lacking for elders with dementia. The language commonly used to describe them is at best demeaning and at worst completely dismissive.

Much of the time, when speaking of Alzheimer's or other dementias, our sympathy is reserved for ourselves as caregivers or as family members. It's all about us, even when the us part of it is also about the care of the other.

To me it seems that much of our difficulty comes about because we don't learn the art and practice of speaking dementia. Once you begin to understand how dementia communication works, you may see a parent's inner being revealed in as much fullness, pain and humanness as your own. Then you become able to see that person in the same depth as you see yourself.

From that time on, it becomes worthwhile to make the effort to stand beside the person with dementia. To stand in shared spirit and communicating feelings.

Family caregivers, by the way, are not alone in assumptions that often nothing much is going on in the person with dementia. Professional caregivers can be just as unseeing and uncomprehending. While family caregivers are often lost in their own struggle of pain, confusion and too much stuff to do, this can be equally true of professionals. We can all fail to see, hear and respond to the deep being of a person with dementia.

These days, medical people are working with patients in deep coma. So, to me it's especially tragic that on the whole we don't try to work with people with dementia.

Even doctors, unfortunately, can be dismissive and cruel. Perhaps because of their own fears of aging, sickness and death. After all, doctors are educated to conquer disease—yet we all die. That's a tremendous judgment on the success or failure of that whole policy of the conquest of disease.

We can also add another oddity here. In the age of 12-step programs, self-development, self-help and support groups, in general caregivers are seldom challenged to face their own issues in the caregiving relationship. Their sense of grief, loss, anger, resentment, bewilderment and pain. It's as if we allow polite assumption that being a caregiver is burden enough. We shouldn't ask them to grow as well.

Well, it's just not enough to leave caregiving as something that just must be borne. We have to make a fuller effort to teach the skills of understanding dementia to caregivers. Lacking those skills and that understanding is precisely WHY life as a caregiver is so difficult. That, allied to whatever personal issues the caregiver brings to caring.

And since the issues of personal pain, difficulty and psychological history tend not to be approached by caregiver organizations, this all too often leaves caregivers half-drowning. It's extraordinary to me that in the 40-plus years that Alzheimer's has been popularly recognized as a health issue, almost no steps forward have been taken to empower caregivers, teach skills and teach the understanding of dementia communication.

Well, the time is now. There can be no more ignoring that real issue in dementia care—the neglect of teaching caregiver skills and the true understanding of how to keep connection with a person with dementia.

Acquiring the tools of knowledge, practicing the care approach and dealing with the personal issues are inextricably mixed. Too few caregivers seem willing to truly look at themselves. They seldom ask themselves if they are actually part of the problem. But that's a very healthy question for us to ask ourselves.

It doesn't mean we're bad people if we are part of the problem. It just means we need more skills, more tools and more insight. It means we have be willing to lay down some of our pain. It means we need to sort out the difference between the issues of dementia and the issues of our own inner being. That's all.

My experience of caregivers is that many are willing to begin to do that. They just haven't been asked to do it enough. And they just haven't been given the right tools. But I wrote this book to ask you to be willing to do two important things:

1. To let go of your own pain;
2. To learn to speak dementia.

If you grow and change in those ways, your life will be easier and your care will be better AND nothing of what you learn will ever be wasted.

Take any issue which causes problems. Short-term memory, for example, as a support group leader, I can't tell you how often a caregiver presents a care problem as "I keep telling him not to.." or "I told her to.."

As any unstressed person could identify, in short-term memory issues, we must assume they will be constant in people with dementia. Not fixable, not retrainable, because they are the result of brain damage that right now cannot be healed.

Therefore, a wise caregiver understands it won't change so there's no point in still trying to hold back the river of forgetfulness. The caregiver who attaches anger or blame to the symptom is not paying attention to self-care. Also not asking himself or herself why exactly they want to be angry.

Having anger is a natural response to loss, fear, stress and too little sleep, but attaching it to someone's else's disease symptom is damaging for both parties. Rather than continue the anger-at-symptom cycle of energy-reducing behavior, a wise caregiver asks what it's all about. In finding the roots of the anger, the caregiver may find peace.

That's why one useful tool for a caregiver is simply to ask, "Why am I letting myself get so angry?"

For most caregivers, an immediate answer is likely to be, "I need sleep."

A deeper answer may also include, "Because this is my mother who didn't care enough for me when I was young," Family difficult, pain and loss mark many caregivers, which is why they seek out caregiving as their healing.

There has been a general neglect of developing the skill of personal insight and the development of care tools. People don't need to die of caregiving—and yet they are. And that's pointless.

People don't become caregivers because they're bad people. Caregivers are good people who often have not been helped sufficiently to care for themselves. In fact, they may have been raised that way—to give their own needs no importance or value—by the very people they're looking after.

So, there we find that terrible match of the uncared-for adult caring for the uncared-for parent who couldn't care well enough in the first place.

In dementia families, we may find that cycle of loss and pain going on down the generations. The great thing about our times is that now we recognize these family patterns. And we are in a time when people want to change them. Plus, we have the tools to do it. In dementia care of a parent, this can be the perfect time to work on that. You can indeed become a great mother to the mother who wasn't so great at mothering you. If you want to.

It's not easy.

That was my journey and it hasn't been easy. But it has been great. And it has brought immense healing to me. Perhaps I've become a better person—at least once or twice a week anyway—but mainly I've become a deeply happier person with a rich spiritual life. And I've learned a lot about putting my well-being right up there on my list.

It's not true that caring for someone with dementia must mean you can't have time to care for yourself. Actually, being a dementia caregiver is like being on the airplane with your little kid.

When accidents happen, you put the oxygen mask on your own face first, then attend to the others. Being a caregiver is like that every day.

So, this book will ask you to care for yourself too. In fact, I'm asking you to make your own care the first major commitment.

If that seems laughably impossible right now, then you're

reading the right book, my friend. Don't be like the angry woman who said to a caregiver group, "I don't have time to care for myself!"

Whether you are a professional caregiver or a family member caring for parent, spouse or other relative, you aren't often asked to seek your own inner development in this journey of caregiving. Not in the average support group, nor the average Alzheimer's or dementia workshop.

We seem to have all-but-forgotten that caregiving is a profound spiritual journey. An emotional growth process that can raise you up and grow your strength and inner being as few others can. Back in history, it was the members of the great spiritual orders who looked after the sick and the dying.

That was not because, being members of those orders, they were supposed to do good deeds—although that is also true. It was because caring for other human beings through illness and even walking to the gates to death beside them is one of the most powerful spiritual and emotional journeys most of us ever undertake.

You'll learn more than in five years of meditating in the wilderness or sitting in a Himalayan cave, that's for sure. That is why it's hard—because it's deep.

I'm not going to teach you the spiritual lessons—you're going to learn your own. Someone's else's dementia condition alone will be your spiritual teacher. I'm going to help you see dementia and understand it better. I'm going to teach you the language of dementia as I've learned so far. And, as always in language learning, we'll start by looking at the culture of de-mentia as it affects those who have the condition.

I'm going to share the tools, coping skills and tricks of the dementia trade as much as I know them. And I'll show you how to see better what is really going on with the person you care for, how to take care of yourself, how to communicate better, how to manage behaviors, how to solve problems and—heavens to Betsy! -- how to have some fun along the way. Because, if you're not having any fun as a caregiver, I never want to be looked after by you, okay?

Now, I don't promise you all your problems will go be solved by this book. For one, thing I'm talking about them, not about you. You're another issue altogether, my friend.

No, here's how dementia caregiving goes. One thing works on Tuesday morning and Friday afternoon, but not on Wednesday nor on Saturday. Nothing always works. Most things work sometimes, or even often, if they're the right things.

Kindness always works somewhat and a sense of humor keeps you sane, although a little healthy nuttiness is always useful in a caregiver.

No-one outside caregiving really understands what we do. No-one understands how much it eats up our life. Tires us out. Makes us eat too much ice cream late at night from loneliness.

**18**

Caregiving is not a task. It is a journey. We learn it step by step. On this journey, we are forced to look deep inside our own hearts. There's no magic key. Just each of us, this vast army, of people caring for people. Learning stuff as we go along. The major work that caregivers do is the work within, on ourselves.

Without that, I promise you, both parties will be praying for death to save them from each other.

Looking after another person touches every part of who we are—all our good and all our bad. That's why it's hard. We have to face some things about ourselves we don't want to see. With me, it was my impatience and my perfectionism, two personality traits notable for achieving absolutely nothing with a person with dementia.

Twenty years have, I like to think, slightly improved that part of me, on a good day. But even now, it's easier for me to tell you how to make things better for yourself, than to always make my things better for me. However, caregiving helped me heal from a happy childhood that was shattered when I was four.

Caring for people with dementia has grown my spirit. It often makes me laugh a whole lot. And you could feel that way about it too, even if it's your Mom or your spouse.

Caregiving is a gift which can give far more than it takes. If you don't know that yet, you will by the end of this book.

Sitting with the dying, for example, is immeasurably difficult but also a time of great radiance. It's not all about loss. It's also about transcendence. It connects us with every other human on the planet. Walk slowly, even once, to the gates of death with another human being and you will never be the same again. But you have to do it, to find that out.

Be realistic about what you can do. If you are constantly overwhelmed, upset and angry, it just means you need help. Be willing to ask yourself, "Does this person need more care than one person can give?" If the answer is yes, then, please make sure to get that help. Remember, two-thirds of all home caregivers die before the person they're caring for.

So, please don't try to do everything alone. No-one will like you better for it. Certainly not your person. Sleep long. Eat well. Love generously. Forgive. Have fun. Be flexible.

Oh yes, plus, always ask an expert how to do something properly because all the sleeping, eating, loving and forgiving in the world doesn't make undies comfortable if a caregiver gets them on you just a little bit wrong.

Most caregiving we do alone. Because of that, it's easy to forget how many of us there are. We are millions. A huge army of humans caring for each other. We're everywhere. In small towns. In hilly cabins. In cities. In every place that Americans live. That's where you find us.

Never forget that. Find the others. Go to support groups. Speak out. Attend meetings. Get what you need.

Because we are out here, I promise you.

*DEMENTIA 101 -- UNDERSTANDING THE BASICS*

Frena Gray-Davidson

## WHAT IS DEMENTIA ANYWAY?

No wonder everyone's confused about dementia. For one thing, dementia itself IS confusing. It's both a bunch of observed behaviors and symptoms, sometimes produced as the side-effect of another condition, and often an illness condition of its own.

A person could have a specific illness dementia—Alzheimer's, Korsakoff's, Pick's, HIV-AIDS, vascular, Lewy Body, fronto-temporal—or dementia resulting from general health conditions such as heart problems, COPD and other lung conditions, liver trouble, cancer or even just the life passage of becoming very old or dying.

21

And then, there is the huge mix of misconceptions, weird ideas and widespread bad publicity about dementia that make it even more confusing.

So, if you're confused right now about dementia— you're right on track. So take a d-e-e-e-p breath and try to relax. There, now. Do it again. Ten times.

Here's a little list of the most common questions confused people ask about dementia:

1. What's the difference between Alzheimer's and dementia?
2. What is dementia?
3. Are people with dementia crazy?
4. How can you tell if someone has dementia?

Just so that you will know those basics, I'll answer those questions briefly. Here goes:

**1.What's the difference between Alzheimer's and dementia?**
Alzheimer's disease is just one dementia. It is the most often

spoken of, but that doesn't mean it is really the most commonly found. There is, as yet, no definitive marker for Alzheimer's disease specific only to Alzheimer's and there is as yet no known cause or cure.

However, it IS the most widely researched disease on the planet right now, by the way. That means you can reasonably hope for the cure to be found soon. The difference between Alzheimer's and other dementias is that *all Alzheimer's IS dementia but NOT all dementia is Alzheimer's*. There are many other dementias, some with their own name and symptoms and others unnamed and diagnosed only by visible symptoms.

### 2. What is dementia?

Dementia is actually an observed group of symptoms, such as serious short-term memory problems, loss of power of reasoning, loss of ability to use rational thinking processes for problem-solving and loss of ability to carry out the usual tasks of everyday living. All this not related to any visible cause, such as having a stroke.

There may also be social issues, such as becoming more isolated, less willing to see friends and family, dropping old social habits and pursuits, becoming fearful of others.

There can also be functional issues of self-care which others notice deteriorating. Poor grooming or looking uncared-for, as a new issue.

The house may also show signs of the same neglect, with food supplies bare, laundry not done and lack of order becoming general.

These are the kinds of changes that make people think an elder has Alzheimer's. This is not necessarily true, however. In reality, they are only signs that something is wrong and that help and intervention is needed.

### 3. Are people with dementia crazy?

People with dementia are NOT crazy. However, it is not unheard for older people who are mentally ill, but have never formerly been diagnosed, to be labeled as having dementia.

That's largely because dementia has been so demonized in our society that we equate it with madness. We assume irrational and acting-out elders do have dementia.

Although accurate diagnosis is improving, it is still not uncommon for mentally-ill elders to be thrown into the Alzheimer's basket. It's as if we say, "Alzheimer's, mental illness, craziness—what's the difference anyway?"

Frankly, that's all part of our societal disrespect for people with dementia and we must all stand up against that kind of discrimination. There's a lot of difference between dementia and mental illness. For one thing, dementia is NOT mental illness. It is a brain-processing issue resulting from deterioration of the actual physical structure of the brain.

On the other hand, seriously mentally-ill elders may have schizophrenia, bipolar disorder or be psychotic and paranoid or may have long-untreated PTSD through war service or child abuse. Seriously mentally-ill elders can literally kill other old people in residential care with them—and sometimes they do.

People with dementia may have occasional interaction issues but generally this is rare and often evoked by poor care handling. And people with dementia can't plan and carry out attacks on others. Planning and remembering the plan are impossible in dementia.

How would a family member know to even seek a diagnosis of mental illness? By assessing the lifelong behavior patterns of an elderly relative and paying attention to warning signs. A parent who has long been secretive, afraid and expressed odd and threatening ideas about outsiders might well be mentally ill.

A lifelong pattern of mood swings from violent and destructive to isolated and depressed might indicate a bipolar condition. Drug or alcohol addiction might suggest the need for mental health diagnosis.

Many addicts are self-medicating more profound afflictions. Don't be afraid because you don't know what's going on. That's why there are experts, to help find out for you.

As a caregiver, I have learned to pay attention to certain catchwords that warned me something else might well be going on with a family member said to have dementia. Phrases like, "Mother's nerves," "Grandma's anger issues" or "Dad's moods" often signal the existence of real and sometimes very serious mental health issues.

It is also possible for a person to have what's called a dual-diagnosis, which would be dementia AND a mental health condition. It's always important to know what exactly is going on, so an assessment from a psychiatrist is important when the question of mental illness is considered. Neurologists deal with brain function, psychiatrists with thinking. So you may well take your family member to see both for a thorough assessment when you're in doubt.

Dementia does not make it impossible for a person to have a peaceful happy life. In fact, some people with dementia become happier because they forget issues which had formerly tormented them. Being cared for, they may feel safer and more emotionally secure than ever before. They may become able to relax for the first time in their lives.

Elders with serious mental illnesses, and I would guess from my own experiences that is about 20 percent of the so-called Alzheimer's population in care facilities, need accurate diagnosis from a psychiatrist, plus appropriate interventions. In care facilities for people with dementia, they may well not get this. The tendency is for facilities to go along with a diagnosis, even a bad one. Whether this is sheer ignorance or money-driven, I can't say. I do know it can be disastrous to mix the two populations, however.

**4. How can you tell if someone has dementia?**

You can't. I can't. Your doctor can't, UNLESS the whole Alzheimer's work-up has been done. The observed behaviors that make others think an old person has dementia could apply to a very wide range of other issues.

That is why the appropriate response to suspected dementia is the full Alzheimer's work-up. Only after that, could a reasonably accurate diagnosis be made. So if you're worried about someone, then take them to their doctor and ask for a referral for a full Alzheimer's work-up.

Do not accept the **mini-mental memory test** as a confirmation of dementia. It isn't.

It only confirms poor memory, which you probably knew anyway. It gives no clue about what causes that memory problem.

From what my support groups tell me, the doctor most resistant to referring patients to an Alzheimer's diagnostic center is an older doctor long-acquainted with the patient. Just remember, NO doctor can diagnose Alzheimer's just by observation. It takes profound investigation. So, insist on referral.

Some people say, "Alzheimer's can't be fixed, so why bother with a work-up?" And that may sound reasonable to you.

However, at least 15 percent of people thought to have dementia actually turn out to have fixable problems of another kind. A further percentage have conditions that can be helped and adjusted, with medications, equipment or procedures. That alone should get you seeking a referral.

Plus, since Alzheimer's is the most researched medical condition in the world today, both treatment and cure remain daily possibilities.

Diabetes was a killer condition until January 11, 1922, when insulin was introduced for common use. Overnight, diabetes became a chronic containable condition, largely controlled successfully with insulin.

That could happen for Alzheimer's and the other dementias too. You'd never get them fixed if you'd never had the work-up done. So that alone makes it worthwhile.

So, I now assume you have had that work-up done and you know your person that you care for has been determined to have dementia, possibly of the Alzheimer's type. Your doctor will have discussed possible medications or modifications that might help problems.

Or, you may be taking a wait-and-see approach and looking at this book anyway. You are very welcome to read my book, but I would still urge you to get a proper and thorough diagnosis done as soon as possible. You have nothing to lose by that, especially if you might in fact be missing out on the chance to get an imbalance or an undetected medical condition helped, treated or cured.

That's why we get the full Alzheimer's work-up.

So, although I do go on to talk about dementia, what it looks like and how we interact with it, you can't diagnose your own person from those descriptions. You still need the diagnosis.

## *Notes to Self*

## WHAT DOES NORMAL DEMENTIA LOOK LIKE?

Here's a check-list for you, so you can figure out whether your person is normal by dementia standards. And why would you want to know that?

Mainly because people may have very bizarre ideas about what dementia-normal looks like. They might therefore overlook signs that something else serious is going on. Again, let me remind you that is not so YOU can diagnose. It is so you can ask a doctor what's going on, okay?

Someone with normal dementia typically does the following:

1. **Forgets some things** or almost everything, about today, yesterday, the last decade, or the last 50 years— it varies.

2. **Forgets lifelong skills** like computing or knitting or whatever.

3. **May call you Mom or Dad** and seem to be living back in childhood time.

4. Puts sheets in the oven to dry them off or other mistaken attempts to misapply once-familiar logic.

5. **Loses everything** or puts it in what you think are odd places .

6. **May wander** around at night.

7. Gets lost while driving, walking or even being in the yard.

8. **Can't follow logical discussion** and may become agitated or upset if pressed.

9. May be upset and fractious when confused or tired.

10. Probably **eats lots of sweet stuff.**

11. **Seems afraid or reluctant to shower.**
12. **Can't find the bathroom** in time and may
    have incontinence episodes.

Remember: Each person does dementia in his or her own way. There are a number of commonly found signs especially short-term memory issues, but these can also be very individual.

It helps if you, as the caregiver, figure out the logic of things, if you can. For example, people may seem to be feeling that they're young and living in their parents' house again. This can seem very disturbing to present-day people—you, for example.

But it's not that strange really. Long-term memory is often surprisingly little-affected by dementia. Nearly all older people, with or without dementia, experience an intensification of long-ago memory. For the person with dementia, this is also true. So your parent may be deeply involved in reviewing the past and also have forgotten which year this is now.

In the short-term memory world, which is today, people with dementia actually forget that they forget. So, they get involved with that long-term memory intensification that most normal elders also experience.

They think about their school days, or living on the family farm, and they feel totally involved in very real-feeling memory recall. They have no short-term memory at work to remind them: "Hey this is now, that was then!" That's why you might get called Mom or Dad. Or they might want to go outside and help with the milking, when they live in the middle of New York City.

It's actually the logical result of their brain damage. It's not hallucination nor delusional thinking. It's also not very useful when we apply the psychiatric jargon of mental illness to a physical wound to brain processing.

So relax and enjoy, rather than get freaked out and weird,

Remember, other people's dementia is not all about you. They don't make you not exist when they feel this is 1926 in Mom and Dad's house. Your feelings are your problem.

In fact, if you'd look at it this way, when they call you Mom or Dad, they are actually signaling to you that a) **you ARE family** and b) **you are important**. That's the dementia memory code talk at work. Give them a break, would you? Please?

The memory is deeply injured in dementia. Brain scans will show you that this is literally true. You can see where the plaques and tangles, or other damage have made the brain unable to process memory-thinking normally.

Therefore, no-one with dementia forgets you deliberately. They don't call you a different name or think you're their Mom to hurt you. You don't cease to exist for them because they got your name wrong.

They haven't stopped relating to you or caring about you. It's just that their brain issues have wounded their memory. So, let go of your feelings of loss and instead really BE with them. Hug, touch, joke, hold and stroke them and forgive what they can't do any more. Stand on their side.

Lots of meaningful love and affection is available to you other than in accurate memory. Make it your special gift to them to forgive and enjoy the moment. I promise you, that will make a powerful difference.

The one who is well is the one who reaches out to and enfolds the wounded one. People have done that for centuries and you can do it too.

## Notes to Self
_____

## How Do You Know When Dementia's Abnormal?

Since dementia has such a bad press, no-one seems surprised by anything. But there are signs that something is wrong that is NOT normal dementia. It's useful to have a few ideas about these and then to make wise decisions when you think enough oddities have arisen to make you question what you're seeing. It's always okay to ask for a referral to an expert—neurological and psychiatric.

Looking through on-line websites, I'm often saddened by families thinking they should put up with extraordinarily disruptive, violent and peculiar behaviors as part of a regular dementia care. This is not so. It's always right to ask for more expert help and for most elders it will be covered by Medicare.

The kinds of behaviors that are unusual include many of the following:

**1. Seeing things that aren't there:**

Often, we need to allow for this conceivably being attributable to vision problems and consequent misinterpretation —such as a shadow of a tree branch being interpreted as a bear. However, your person might really be hallucinating.

This does NOT include being visited by dead relatives, however. That is a normal phenomenon for most elders, especially when nearing death or actually dying. Whatever your opinion about it, that's a fact as a well-known phenomenon which is not a mental health issue.

**2. Thinks the television is talking to them;**

**3. Fears intruders to an extravagant degree;**

**4. Signs of paranoid thinking;**

5. Has **extensive periods of raging,** even all night;
6. **Reluctant** to see family members;
7. **Won't change clothes;**
8. **Refuses all medication** for fear reasons;

Caregivers should just be aware that this person has a very **elevated fear level,** and may be **psychiatrically disturbed.** Keep an eye on this, make notes and if it increases steadily or suddenly and dramatically, seek medical advice from a psychiatrist.

Many people with dementia are afraid, not surprisingly. Just be aware of this and up the security and comfort level for your person. If they feel safe with you, fear symptoms can subside and possibly dissipate completely.

Be respectful, don't badger or reproach them for their symptoms. This may well help them to relax and not be so anxious. The more anxious and nervous you are, the more they will be. **Agitation, fear and anxiety are all contagious** in both directions unless one direction takes action. That's you.

**Behaviors Needing Further Investigation:**
1. **Night turmoil** which continues for hours;
2. **Night terrors;**
3. **Extremely fearful** and reclusive;
4. **Calls police frequently;**
5. **Accuses neighbors** of bad behaviors, when untrue;
6. **Hits out;**
7. **Fears poisoned food** and drink;
8. **Plans and carries out attacks;**
9. **Hears voices,** at silent times;
10. **Feels pursued** by enemies;
11. **Relives trauma;**
12. **Moves heavy furniture** around at night, with construction of barricades.

Now, I'm not trying to diagnose anybody here. Just really encouraging doubtful family members to INSIST on getting expert consultation with a psychiatrist. A family should not

31

be trying to live with a person who has serious mental illness without a lot of extra help, support and perhaps medication for that person.

When a family is left with an erroneous and careless diagnosis of dementia, they will often struggle on for years, assuming that the difficult and challenging issues of their family member is normal dementia. That is a debilitating and destructive process for everyone. And it can be dangerous in its outcome too.

Dementia care of real people with real dementia is not like these lists we've just looked at. It's not usually filled with the terror, distortion of reality and struggle that caring for a seriously mentally-ill parent with no help from psych meds and psych expertise is likely to be. It does not have extended violence.

I'm not saying it's always fun and easy, because it's not. But it really can be fun and often has reward and interest going on, with a real sense of being able to make deep heart contact with that person you care for.

Getting the right diagnosis for mental illness in elders takes determination. Even now, too many doctors are still likely to tell you that bizarre or threatening behavior is "just Alzheimer's" or "normal dementia", and this is absolutely not true. Don't accept that. Get to a psychiatrist.

First, trust your own sense that something beyond dementia is going on here. However, I have always found that a family does in fact—kind of, sort of, deep down—have that sense about a mentally-ill elder. What they sometimes lack is the courage or knowledge of how to go further.

However, it's easier than you think. Under Medicare, you can go to your parent's doctor, with an outline of what you see in list form, and ask for a referral for your person to go to see a psychiatrist. If you think your person will refuse, explain to them that this will help with getting their medications looked at. On the appointment day, don't mention psychiatrist or make a big deal of anything.

Just get in the car and drive there and walk into the office with your person. Although many families have told me their person would refuse to go to a psychiatrist, when you deal with it less directly, I have not known anyone yet whose parent turned round and stormed out.

Very often, it is we ourselves who have to relax, step down the tension and let go of trying to argue someone into things. Just make the arrangements, keep them low-key, allow plenty of time and good luck!

I promise you, it will help to go to a psychiatrist. A lot. It will help your person to have some peace and relief from fear in their last years. It can also bring back the person who was meant to be living in that body. As a friend of mine said, when the family finally had a diagnosis of bipolar condition for their mother and appropriate and successful medication, "I finally met the mother I never knew I had."

Not sure if Grandma's mentally ill or just her mean old self? You don't have to know, What you need to know is: how can the family help Grandma?

No family member should undertake care of an elder when no-one knows what's wrong. If other family members are trying to make you do that, tell them sweetly and insistently, "We need to know what Grandma's medical status is, before we plan her care."

Stick to your ground. Remind them she can't get the best care from all of them when no-one knows what ails her. That needs a medical expert, not a collection of family stories.

## Notes to Self

## DEMENTIA AND HALLUCINATIONS

You will hear people, including your doctor, say that people with dementia often experience hallucinations.

I've worked with many people with dementia and I'm still not convinced that what most of them experience is actually an hallucination. A lot of the so-called hallucinations are clearly our misinterpretation of dementia-talk, plus interpretation-confusion in the person with dementia.

We caregivers can also just plain be insensitive about what it's really like to be subject to the severe memory changes, cognitive losses and strong emotional processes of dementia. It is so much easier to say there is one simple word to describe all this—hallucination. But that's often really our way of saying to the person with dementia, "You're wrong."

And that is hardly ever a good way to get someone feeling you're on their side. After all, does hearing from someone that you're wrong often work well for you?

The other problem with using the word hallucination is that it frightens caregivers unnecessarily, making them think their person must be crazy.

Don't forget that people with dementia are often compensating by making up stuff to fill their memory gap. And they don't feel they're making it up either. It's not deliberate story-making. It's just a sanity saving device to fill the huge memory gaps and losses.

Elders often have sight and hearing deficits, so we don't know how often they misunderstand what they hear and see. If Grandma sees a shadow out of the window and says it's a man

34

going by, is that hallucination? I'd make that a "doubtful."

As people not yet operating with broken short-term memory PLUS the intensification of long-term memory typical of old age, we really don't know how this is experienced but we could try to imagine.

If you are in long-term memory, living in a past moment with your mother, with the intensification that you don't realize is going on, you may report the conversation you had with your mother.

"Mom told me she's not doing so well with her arthritis now," says your elderly Mom, whose elderly Mom is long-dead.

You may assume she's hallucinating. Yet, strictly, she isn't hallucinating. She's misinterpreting more than hallucinating. Therefore, this is not appropriately classified as hallucinating either.

Don't think I'm just trying to excuse everything. Not so. I'm trying to encourage caregivers to be more discerning about the experiences of people with dementia. Having hallucinations is a very different and I'd say more medically serious event than misinterpreting or just plain forgetting that we forget.

You see, the problem with lack of discernment is that it is always the person with dementia who gets the heavy meds, okay? And heavy meds can and do kill a lot of elders.

In fact, recent studies from Europe, Canada and the USA show that about one-third of all elders given anti-psychotic medications—usually inappropriately, by the way—are killed by them. That is why I labor the issue of we caregivers becoming much more discerning about what is really going on in elders with dementia.

Elders, with dementia and without, experience visitations from dead relatives. There is no useful general agreement on how to classify this. According to who you listen to, it's hallucination, a spiritual experience, wishful thinking or seeing dead people. Just understand that such visitations are known to everyone who works in the Hospice movement.

In fact in our society right now, there can be no consensus

on what to call these experiences. Even Christians who would claim to believe in life after death don't apparently believe that loving (but dead) family members would reach out to the suffering living.

So I suggest you call these "around-death-experiences" or "visitation events". Whatever you call it, you can be clear in assuming this is not appropriately classified as hallucination.

Most of the elders I have know who allegedly had dementia AND hallucinations were people who turned out to have serious mental illness. But there are exceptions. People with Lewy Body dementia often have interesting hallucinations involving color and unexpected appearances. For example, a friend of mine reports her grandmother used to see colored rabbits playing in her kitchen. They were purple and red and pink and she knew they were not real.

"I know they're not really there, honey," she said, "But oh, I so enjoy them!"

In one of my support groups a wife reported that her husband had recently been seeing little green men out in the cactus patch beyond their property. He was aware that it was odd to see them and he was amused by his own experience. Very oddly, two months later, a different couple came to a meeting and again it was the husband who was seeing little green men out in the desert. I was intrigued to find out that both couples lived in the same part of town.

Make of that whatever you care to.

Don't be upset when your person mentions seeing things you know they didn't. If they see a beloved dead family member, just say what a comfort that must be.

If they say they saw Dad last night, be friendly and casual and say something like, "Oh, how did he look?"

If Grandma sees a bear in the garden, take a little walk together to see if it's still there and chat about it. (If you actually live in bear country, don't do this.)

Just remember: there's nothing unusual in being visited by dead relatives.

Only take action if your person is terrified by recurrent visions. Then you do get a psychiatrist's appointment.

Oh yes, one more thing: did your person start seeing things after starting a new medication? If so, it's likely to be the meds. Many mood control, anxiety and tranquilizer meds do really strange things to people with dementia. They may give them real hallucinations, make them scream regularly for no known reason or turn them into falling-down zombies.

Check the internet to see if there are more reports of this. Even if there aren't, go back to the doctor for a change of medication. Or, if it isn't life-saving, see if your doctor will go along with "waiting and seeing" while not using that med.

## *Notes to Self*

## When Does Dementia Really Begin?

It is obvious to me, from everything I have now experienced in my 20 years of dementia care, that dementia starts at least 20 years before anyone outside the experience notices. Maybe even longer. Maybe, as some have suggested, it really is some genetic tendency you're born with that just takes a long time or the triggering events to develop. Like arthritis. Or heart disease.

That I don't know—but  medical science will be able to tell us more clearly how or why  it happens as research continues. I do know that dementia takes time to develop. During that time, especially in the years just before it begins to outwardly manifest, people experience its encroachment into their lives.

Since they seldom talk about it to others, I call this the **Secret Dementia**. The Secret Dementia is known only to the sufferer. These days, when the term dementia is much more widely known and the word Alzheimer's much more widely spoken, people may identify it in themselves. In the past, they identified it only in the ways in which they experienced what was going on. During the years of the Secret Dementia, people may experience any of the following, or even individual symptoms peculiar to themselves:

**The possible signs of the Secret Dementia:**

1. **Periods of short-term memory** dysfunction often described as "absence". It's the loss of recall that they're describing, a sense of realizing they have a gap of hours they can't recall. A sort of very short-term amnesia;

2. **Loss of cognitive ability** for a period of time, usually fairly short, but recurring.

A woman in her early forties told me about her experiences of getting into her car and looking down at the gas and brake pedals, suddenly aware that she had no idea what to do.

She consciously made herself relax, with slow breathing, and gradually the knowledge returned.

**3.** In a more fearful person, these episodes cause tremendous terror reactions which may manifest outwardly as **inexplicable rage** or the sudden manifestation of **heavy alcohol use;**

**4. Unusual emotional outbreaks** may begin to occur—sudden weeping, loss of emotional control, wild accusations of a kind that might sound paranoid but are actually extreme fear reactions;

**5. Baseless accusations** of neighbors stealing, people breaking in, intruders threatening, may mark this period of time also.

Since these are varied and extremely individual behaviors which could mark a lot of health conditions—from brain tumors to paranoid schizophrenia, as well as possible dementia—the only thing an observer could conclude is that something is wrong and help is needed.

Perhaps if you already knew that familial dementia was an issue in the life of this person, you might hone in on that, but even then—remember that research has not really established consistently useful data in that field. Just assume something is wrong and see if this person could be persuaded to go to the doctor.

Again, no matter what the family history has been, you cannot make a diagnosis from apparent memory issues and some confusion.

Few people are both willing and able to share their sense of disquiet at their own dysfunction with other family members, but some do.

One woman said to her husband one day, "I don't know what's going on but there's something very wrong with me. I just can't do these things any more. You're going to have to."

After medical investigation, she was diagnosed as having a dementia of the Alzheimer's type. And her husband did indeed begin to take over the tasks that had once been hers. Their situation was unusual in that she was very open and honest.

Even though almost everyone knows about Alzheimer's now, people are still seldom that honest with each other. Denial is still the most usual thing that happens. Our society has demonized Alzheimer's, made it so fearful and awful that no-one wants to be around it, not even people who have it.

Maybe we could start to think about how we need to change all that and have it be just one more illness that we could learn how to deal with.

What do you think?

### *Notes to Self*
_____

## WHEN DEMENTIA IS INVISIBLE

Most people think dementia starts when you see it. You know, with memory glitches that are consistent, serious and obvious to everyone. With being unable to run daily life. Not keeping things going the way you used to.

Everyone knows that these might be pointers to dementia — although we'd also be smart to realize it could also be other illnesses, depression, loss of sight and hearing ability or other issues. Lots of issues manifest the way we think dementia does. But what about that time period in which there is no outer manifestation of dementia?

41

We don't hear much about that. I call the Invisible Stage in dementia, including Alzheimer's dementia.

How do I even know there is an Invisible Stage, since by the name alone it's—well—invisible? I know because of documentation that I noted in three separate people that I cared for in my first years as a caregiver.

One woman was a 79-year-old, Hannah, who had won her college degree at 64 but at 74 had been diagnosed as having Alzheimer's. Since she was the first person I had ever looked after with Alzheimer's, I was very curious about the whole development of the condition—as I still am.

Hannah had kept voluminous diaries all her life and her family agreed to let me read them as a way of knowing who she once had been. I was also, however, looking for clues. I just felt intuitively that this was not a disease that started only when outsiders could see it. That didn't make sense to me at all.

I found the clue I was searching for in the diary she kept after her husband's death. She was about 50 at the time he died and I found a passage in which she talked of "this terrible absent-mindedness of mine." That was the first mention of anything that might possibly be construed as the beginnings of dementia. She had written it 24 years before her diagnosis.

A second clue came from the life of Sheila Moon, a well-known Jungian analyst, poet and writer profoundly interested in Navajo culture. When I came into her life, she was already deeply affected by dementia but still able to talk. She was really a mentor for me in seeing the great journey within the journey of losses. I looked for clues in her published writings.

In her book, "Dreams of A Woman", I found two references to a particular time period in which she had two big meaningful dreams. In one, she was told by a doctor that she had an irreversible brain disease. In another, she met a spiritual figure in a long white robe. He said she would be asked to join a special order in which she would be of the world but not in the world.

That's one of the best definitions of dementia I've ever read, by the way. She was in her early forties then and would not be diagnosed until her early 70s.

The third clue came from the life of Rebecca. I cared for her in her late 80s. She had been a medical social worker and in fact ran the social work department of a large Bay Area hospital until her retirement at 65. She was diagnosed with Alzheimer's in her 80s.

After her death, I helped clear her apartment and I found in her underwear drawer—where, as we know, all the secrets are kept—an old file folder. It had in it a series of articles on yellowing newsprint, all about memory problems. The articles dated back to her forties.

I understood just by those three examples that dementia began growing inside a person decades before it ever showed on the outside. Only that person knew that something within them was changing.

Think of that long loneliness.

## NORMAL WEIRD DEMENTIA STUFF

A lot of people are so confused about how dementia affects someone that this often causes tension, stress and frustration for caregivers. Sometimes, caregivers know the names of symptoms but don't quite realize how those symptoms will manifest.

In 15 years of running caregiver support groups, I hear the same complaints over and over about the perceived bad behaviors of those with dementia. Yet the things complained about are the normal symptoms everyone has.

I've never quite established for myself whether these caregivers honestly can't accept the symptoms of their family member or whether they really don't understand the normal manifesting of serious short-term memory problems. Probably a bit of both, is my guess.

43

So, I'm listing here some of the things that may look or sound odd, but which are very normal signs of dementia being present. If you find yourself getting enraged by these, then that is the sign that you need to take better care of yourself. As caregivers we MUST take responsibility for our own feelings and our own shortcomings.

We must NOT give in to becoming martyrs because that is a horrible way to treat another family member. Especially one suffering from a debilitating and permanently damaging illness. So, if that is you, then don't spill over into guilt—another useless emotion. Instead, design the care for yourself that you need. Sleep schedule, time-off schedule, good food and friendship of others. If you don't know where to find those others, start with a caregiver support group.

So here's my list, and it is by no means comprehensive.

**Weird Things Normal to Dementia:**

### 1. Noun Loss:

It's normal for people with dementia to be unable to bring your name to mind. It doesn't mean they hate you. It means they have dementia, which is a physical deterioration of the brain, especially in the short-term memory storage areas.

This loss may extend to being unable to identify the cat as a cat, for example. Again, due to brain affliction, in some people the connection between noun and object may be lost.

So, you could say, "Mom, could you put the light on?" And Mom may not know what the word "light" connects with. So she won't.

Don't get mad at her. Instead improve your own communication. When you use the word "light", that's when you also point to the light switch. This is called cuing, which is a way to give more clues to the person with dementia;

### 2. Calendar Loss:

I know you think you came into the world knowing the day, date, time and year, but you didn't. You learned that. In dementia, people unlearn that.

They live in the year they think they're in. And that will often be the year they emotionally need to be in. Probably in their childhood or youth. Maybe later. Even though time confusion is a product of dementia, nevertheless people with dementia can and are still doing the great work of life review that most other elders do.

They spend their time where the work of memory needs to be done. Usually with parents and childhood and the important things that happened. Sometimes also later with other traumas and joys. Support this work. Be interested. Ask questions, be kind, pass the Kleenex and never tell them to cheer up. Support grief and you will find this person can finally move through it. It's a magnificent task , sitting as witness for life stories.

## Making Up Stories:

Doctors call this confabulation and sometimes judgmental family members who don't at all understand dementia call it "telling lies."

Me, I call it staying sane. You try living in a world where you can't recall yesterday or who these people are around you or your daily routine.

I see the stories people tell about what they did as setting a fence of sanity around themselves to reduce the stress of all that loss. I enjoy it. It's a survival mechanism.

People fill their lives with what they feel would be the norm for them. Meeting a friend for lunch, going shopping, attending church or synagogue, playing cards with the girls.

If these filled someone's life before dementia, they will continue to fill them in the imaginary recall of dementia.

Interestingly, studies on people with dementia show that they genuinely feel they still do what they used to and see the people they used to see. So they have an emotional satisfaction based upon this false impression of daily life. The result of that is they suffer less depression and sense of isolation than do elders who don't have dementia but have lost their former social life due to other kinds of infirmity.

That's another reason not to be mad at your Mom for inventing an interesting life for herself.

So, when your sister telephones Mom and Mom tells your Sis that, yes, she's been out to lunch and then went shopping with friends and she's doing just fine—and you know none of this is true—don't be mad at Mom. Mom's making a healthy adjustment, in a dementia way.

If you feel mad at Mom for covering up in this way, I bet you need some time off and a few days away, don't you? And, of course, you also need to stick it to your sister who doesn't believe your tales of how poorly Mom is doing and how much work goes into her care.

So, don't get mad. Get even. And do it the caregiver way. Tell your sister you need a weekend or a week off and ask when could she come?

When she does come, leave without giving her your destination and keep your cell phone turned off. But do check your messages because you aren't completely irresponsible, are you? And enjoy having your vacation. I guarantee she'll never again think you're exaggerating.

From what I've seen in care facilities, it seems that the less a person has going on in their life, the more extravagant the stories they tell. Old women in long-term care will tell you they were married seven times and had 21 children, though they were actually married once and have one daughter who never visits.

**4. Wandering:**

You and I call this walking and we can do it any darn time we choose. Your Aunt Esther in the Memory Care facility is called a wanderer because there they don't even have a safely enclosed walking path for their residents.

Wandering is what people with dementia do to self-medicate their anxiety and stress. They may also be in search of the way out of the building. Or maybe it's a more metaphorical journey in search of time past.

Whichever, a wanderer still needs a walking program. Someone has to organize that for them. You know who that's likely to be, don't you?

But it doesn't have to be you who takes them. Often a kind neighbor or an interested high school student or church member will be happy to take your aged restless Mom for a careful walk.

Just be sure to give full and clear instructions for this. And perhaps also conduct the first couple of walks yourself as a model for your volunteer.

Sometimes wanderers are perfectly happy with a car ride instead of a walk. Then up their involvement in the tasks of life—safe and easy household chores, helping you cut out coupons, whatever, as long as you aren't attached to the results.

Wandering, restlessness and boredom are often inter-connected. Even a person with dementia is not usually satisfied with sitting around doing nothing all the time. After all, would you be?

It doesn't hurt to check into any local day activity or day care programs for those with dementia. Most people do pretty well with these. Don't ask them if they want to go and don't feel guilty when they show initial reluctance. Just get them there and try it out, because if it does work, it's a great gift for both of you.

**5. Eating funny:**

Mom only wants to eat candy, ice-cream, cake and cookies. She needs supervision and digestive enzymes to enable her food to send those vitally-needed sugars to the brain. Make sure her doctor agrees (but they have no bad side effects and do help digestion to really work properly);.

P.S. None of those essential brain sugars are to be found in ice cream or cookies—wouldn't you just know it?

Mom doesn't want her green food to touch her yellow food. If you want her to eat—and you do—you'll just pay attention to what she wants. Try little meals often. Make the food bright, small, interesting and tasty. Step up the flavor a lot because she is losing the ability to taste and smell food. That's often why people with dementia don't eat much. The sensory stimulation has gone.

Dad is reluctant to eat. Try making smoothies, or giving him a plate of sweet fresh fruit with little chunks of cheese to chew, tender buffalo wings, stuff he can eat with his fingers.

Remember, not all food has to be eaten at the table—and, by the way, do you sit down and eat with your person? Because you should. Company stimulates eating. Sit together on the sofa and eat finger food while you watch Oprah, Ellen, John Wayne or a football match.

**Eating priorities:**

At the dementia point in someone's life, you just want this person to eat. Good or bad food is not even the issue now. Health munchies don't fix dementia, alas, though possibly they might

47

have prevented it in the first place.

So give your person what they'll eat, other than the sugar-rush stuff. Often, an old-time recipe will work well. What I call "Heartland eating". Meat-oriented dishes, weak coffee and white bread—if that's what this person will eat, go for it. Unless they have diabetes, put back the sugar, the fat, the butter and the caffeine because these are stimulants for taste and appetite.

Forget the salads and the fish, unless your person wants those and will eat them. Put back the eggs, the fruit pies and those ghastly old-fashioned soft drinks. You need to get those calories in them. You also need to put the food on their plate and serve it up that way—don't invite them to help themselves because they'll probably only take tiny portions.

If you're dealing with a sugar junkie, don't buy those ice cream bars or popsicles, unless you plan to padlock the freezer.

Your path is best walked between your wish for their healthy eating and their inclination to eat. Go with what will get them eating.

## *Notes to Self*

## How Dementia Begins

This is how normal dementia usually works, although we must never forget the magic mantra of dementia care: **everyone does dementia in his or her own way.**

The first noticeable thing that happens is that gradually you lose the ability to access your short-term memory. You know this long before anyone else notices. That's because it's a long slow process.

By the time others notice, you have probably been unable to retain short-term memories for some years. Probably in that time, you have also begun to lose nouns, especially names.

One woman told me, "When Dad was finally diagnosed with Alzheimer's, I realized that he hadn't called any of us by name for years. It was all Sweetie, Honey, Son—like that."

Having short-term memory damage means you don't remember yesterday at all. You may not even remember five minutes ago. You well may have forgotten or become unclear about the last ten years. It varies from person to person.

That's pretty frightening for anyone. It makes you feel unsafe, insecure, alone. You may react to these feelings in different ways. Some are angry and fearful, others depressed. Some withdraw from human contact. Others take to drink. These are all emotional reactions to the terror that memory damage causes inside you.

As if that weren't bad enough, growing damage to the part of your brain that does cognitive thinking begins to affect you too. It's not that you're becoming stupid. Or that your I.Q. has diminished. It's that you can't retain the steps in thinking.

Before you were ill, your wife would say, "Honey, I need to write a check for $500 for the property taxes before the end of the month or we'll be in trouble," and you heard, remembered and understood everything she said.

Once the damage to your brain affects the once-easy flow of thought information, your wife's sentence might be heard in this way. "Honey, I need [forgotten] $500 for the [forgotten] or we'll be in trouble."

Aware that you don't understand, you react angrily to what you think was said. "I'm not made of money. You're over-spending. I'm not giving you anything!" you yell, refusing to hand over the checkbook.

This is the very beginning step in learning dementia. Caregivers need to develop a deeply compassionate sense of empathy for people whose very brains are betraying them.

50

We need to understand the terror, confusion and desolation that can sweep over them every time they are reminded they can't remember stuff and every time they hear information or questions they just can't follow.

Imagine if it really was you. Maybe you're pretty bad at math. A rotten cook. Lousy at the computer. But you can remember your day and your yesterday. You can retain a whole sentence in your memory in a conversation. You're able to take part in social life without being terrified you'll give yourself away.

Now imagine this. You're a Nobel Prize Winner. You ran the Opera House of a glittering world-renowned city. You're a famous film star, a writer, a poet, a renowned Jungian. And you can't remember what someone just said to you. And you have no idea who they are.

Once you have dementia, all the things that once were part of your very structure are no longer there for you. You may forget your whole last twenty years, including all your attainments. You have lost your operating power, because memory, intellectual organization and life experience give that to us.

For the rest of us who don't have dementia, this is where we begin to learn to speak dementia. Before we ever say a word, we have to understand the losses that people with dementia are forced to live with, every day.

Then we have to step up beside them. Not in pity, but in honest admiration of how they manage to face the average day. Then we walk with them on their day's journey, so they can be more and their fear and loneliness can be less.

## *Notes to Self*

## LEARNING DEMENTIA:

It's always surprising to me when caregivers don't learn dementia basics. Without that, we can never create care which helps people with dementia to feel safe. When we don't do that, we create all kinds of difficulties, from behavior problems to fear-related violence. And it's our fault.

People with dementia need a lot of care, but they are seldom violent unless they feel threatened. When we haven't learned dementia basics, they do feel threatened. So let's consider what are the basics of dementia.

**Dementia Basics:**

1. People with dementia **forget** a lot;
2. Because they forget a lot, they feel **insecure and scared**;
3. Because they're afraid, we need **slow and gentle interactions** with them;
4. **Arguing doesn't work** with dementia;
5. **Logic doesn't work**;
6. **Ordering people around** doesn't work;
7. **Kindness works**;
8. **Humor works**;
9. **Heart connection** works;
10. **Persuasion**, **invitation** and **suggestion** can each work occasionally, regularly or always. Depending on whatever.

**Five Important Facts About Dementia:**

1. People with dementia are **NOT crazy**;

2. **Short-term memory** loss means starting each day anew;

3. When people with dementia **like** you, they feel they **know** you;

4. **Kindness** helps create trust;

5. **Trust** helps eliminate difficult behaviors.

No-one becomes a non-person, having dementia. People lose reliable access to their former life. They lose abilities, but they still have many of the same characteristics. Often, they do not lose their past at all and may have very accurate recall.

**Everything they were is still somewhere within.** Maybe they can reach it sometimes. Often, a good caregiver who gets to know their person well can evoke who they were.

An old woman who has forgotten she used to play piano might play if you place her hands upon the piano keys. It's only her head that's forgotten. Her hands can still play. A dancer may still dance. It's our job to help find out what remains whole.

As caregivers, we can often help replace empty space in a dementia life with old joys. The woman who can no longer make quilts might love to color in coloring books. And you don't have to use those awful kids' coloring books. Dover Books have a wonderful selection of adult coloring books. Plus, that is likely to bring the same calm and achievement she used to know.

People with dementia do things oddly, not because they're stupid, but because they forget the steps in-between they used to know. As caregivers, we can fill in those in-between steps for them. Then they can do something that brings them relief and comfort.

Very often, their level of security and emotional ease depends very much on how we care for them. Our bad day can be hell for them. Our little meanness takes all chance of love that day away from someone whose only hope of love we are.

I'm sure that you don't neglect or abuse the ones you look

after—do you? But do you fully face your responsibility to be the bearer of love? Do you act with respect? Are you kind? If you're not, because you had a fight with your husband or your teenage daughter, then the people you look after will pay for your bad mood all day long.

The best thing we can do, quite often, is to stop pretending. Your people are your prisoners. That's the truth. So, please, leave your troubles aside and welcome them into your heart. Don't have your care be a prison sentence in a tough jail. Instead. make it full of kindness and moments of humor and affection. And, while you're there, love yourself too. Please.

## *Notes to Self*

## UNDERSTANDING DEMENTIA:

For me, one of the most profound and surprising processes we witness in the person with dementia is the heart journey towards finding peace.

Yet, it is also often totally misunderstood, misinterpreted or — amazingly—not even noticed by family and caregivers. So, let's all notice from now on. Watch out for these examples of the process at work.

Your Mom, or your favorite resident, doesn't seem to be very present at all. She is absent, as if absorbed somewhere else. Is this her illness or what? I choose "what".

This person really is somewhere else. My guess? In childhood or youth years, in their parental home, in whatever geographical place that was. So, for example, here you are: Arizona, 2011. Your person? Also in Arizona 2011, right there, with you. In reality, however, she's living in 1926 South Dakota, with Mama and Daddy. She's ten-years-old.

Uh oh, you think medically to yourself, "She's deluded, hallucinating, crazy, disturbed, psychotic."

To which I reply, somewhat sharply, "Get a grip, will you?"

Firstly, how on earth do you think people with short-term memory could get this day, date and time right anyway? They can't. They indeed do not remember what day, date and time this is and therefore they don't know the geography either. All of this is merely a natural and rational result of short-term memory loss.

So, meanwhile, what are they doing? They are doing the Great

Life Review, silly. They're examining life with Mama and Daddy. Re-experiencing, re-examining, making sense of all that happened. Considering losses and joys, trauma and delights. Experiencing the life again, but this time bringing to it all their own life experience.

I can't emphasize enough that this is an emotion-based processing, not linear memory recall, so it is entirely possible for the person with dementia to do.

Y̶ou wonder, are they hallucinating, being delusional or crazy? To which the answers are: No, no, and no. There are two reasons why people visit the past with such deep involvement. One is that short-term memory damage means there is no memory cue for day, date and place. Two, is that the intensity of their memory experiences creates almost a flashback. It feels real. It feels real because the emotions feel real.

Typically, in our judgmental attitude towards the experiences of elders with dementia, we think that's kind of nuts. Yet, if you re-experience a deep sense of loss when your latest romance shrivels and dies, you simply experience it. You don't judge yourself.

So let's bring the understanding and non-judgment we like for ourselves to the inner life of our grandmothers and grandfathers, our parents and our spouses and quit the judging.

That judging does nothing to help us feel empathy for them. So, let's dump the attitude and bring on the heart.

This is what I've learned from my work with elders. I have done years of two kinds of work which are at opposite ends of the elder experience. I've led hundreds of Life Story Writing seminars and classes for elders.

I've also been a 20-year caregiver for elders with dementia. Two entirely different groups of elders. Yet, they share one thing— almost without exception, both groups experience a deep intensification of memory emotion. They emotionally re-experience the powerful events of their past. This happens to elders with all their mental faculties and elders with severe dementia.

Therefore, I conclude that **deep memory intensification is a feeling-related form of recall, powered by emotions and body response, not by memory-linked intellectual calendar process.**

That's the explanation for why your Mom thinks she's living home with her Mom. That's why your Dad keeps talking about his little brother drowning before his eyes when he was ten. They do it because there is **memory-work** to be done. The human heart seeks resolution and peace before death. It's the sacred journey of old age.

This intensification of memory seems to start in the late 50s and deepens with age. That emotional deepening of memory work is what makes it profound and real and able to change us into more centered, less trivial people.

It happens in old age with or without dementia. And that's why our elders with dementia seem absorbed and far away sometimes. They have just been dwelling in the very distant and meaningful past.

Go easy and welcome them back respectfully. And ask questions. We have had so little respect for people with dementia, alas, that we have not even considered asking them about their own thoughts, feelings or wishes.

But we could. We could say, "You seemed very far away just now. Where were you?"

You might get some wonderful answers.

## *Notes to Self*
_____

## How Dementia Memory Works

M ost dementia comes about through physical deterioration of the brain. Certain areas are especially targeted and people lose abilities controlled by those areas.

The most obvious, as you also know, is the ability to remember in the short-term. The phrase "**short-term memory loss**" is not as exact or universal in meaning as you might hope. It has quite variable meanings, according to each individual affected by it. Short-term might be minutes, days, months, a few years or many years.

One forgets the answer to a question, then asks it again. Most people forget yesterday, but might remember a special yesterday. A visit from someone beloved. A new pet maybe.

The eventual range of short-term memory loss might extend for years. One woman forgot the whole marriage to her second husband. She only remembered her first. Memories are embedded not only in the brain calendar computer, but also in emotional impact. Whether wonderful or terrible.

A woman recalls clearly the joyful birth of her first baby. Another woman reacts fearfully as if her father were still around to abuse her. A man recalls his little brother drowning in front of him. These are all memories embedded by emotional impact. The difficulty for family members is that they may then interpret memory loss to be emotional rejection. As in, "My father doesn't even know me."

Actually, their father may well emotionally "know" but is prevented by dementia from getting the right noun out. The loss of proper nouns—otherwise known as your name—for names, is merely dementia. The loss of more and more nouns is also merely dementia.

The whole emotional and psychological shaping of human life tends to be that early life makes the biggest impact, for good or bad. That memory is laid down so deep that little can displace it, other than major brain injury. That is also why an elder is drawn back to that early deep territory—parents, home, belonging, fear or joy.

Both elders with dementia and elders with great memory and excellent health are drawn to spend a lot of time in that territory.

It's not useless dwelling on the past, as uncomprehending people sometimes think. It is the great coming to terms with what happened in a life and how we transcend pain, make sense of people, confront our losses and turn our minds to the coming of death. It is the Great Life Review.

Let's face it, folks, if we all did that before extreme old age, then I dare say that we wouldn't make so many stupid and damaging mistakes in our lives. Better late than never, though. To me, the fascinating aspect of that great memory work is that people with dementia also do this. They do it differently, because they have dementia, but they do it.

You've heard them, but you've dismissed it. You didn't know what you heard. You heard an old woman, a demented old man, talk about living back on the prairie. About Mama and Father. About people dying of scarlet fever. That was it. The great work of memory, done even in dementia.

It's a great journey of the soul that even dementia can't steal from you. And you, as a caregiver—what can you do to help? You can listen. And respond with support. That's all it takes.

I don't know about you, but it makes me feel humble that the soul always does its journey. That we can count on that.

59

## WHAT DOES DEMENTIA EAT?

We often see big changes in how people eat once they have dementia. They may eat tiny amounts, or 6 ice-cream bars in one sitting. They may seem to lose appetite and have no enthusiasm for food. They may lose concentration while eating and seem to forget about it.

How can we help as caregivers?

Well, we can become familiar with some of the many ways that people with dementia may change in their eating styles. Let's take a look at the factors that affect eating.

**Why Don't People With Dementia Eat?**

**1. Changes in sense of taste and smell:**

The sense of smell is entirely lost in about 95 percent of people with dementia and this reduces the interest of food to a significant degree—as it would for you. Think about when you last had a really heavy cold that stuffed up your nose—food just didn't seem so tempting, did it?

Far from needing a bland diet, elders, with and without dementia, need a diet stepped up in taste, flavor and eye appeal. Of course, dietary health issues have to be respected, but salt, sweet and spicy tastes appeal.

Unless there is real medical reason not to, add butter, olive oil, honey, sugar, salt and flavorings to food. Tea and coffee is often much better caffeinated, raising the spirits and giving an energy boost.

**2. Changes in perception of food attractiveness:**

People may have developed preferences they can't express. They may want different foods not to touch each other. They may dislike textures of various kinds.

We need to be very attentive to these possibilities and experiment to see how we can overcome reluctant eating.

It's not so strange either—think about how an three-year-old also has such preferences. I don't think dementia makes people childish, but it may force them to live more simply, as children do while they're learning the world.

People with dementia are unlearning and may revisit earlier stages of development. It seems to be part of human development that may recur in elders with dementia.

Since nagging won't make elders eat, try doing what they want instead. Much better!

3. Brain changes affecting sight. Sometimes, only one side of the plate may be noticed, leaving the other untouched . This might well be due to a small stroke, or visual losses or who knows what? So, just turn that plate around with a kindly reminder that they might like to eat that food too. And if they don't or won't, that's okay.

4. **Brain changes affecting spatial relationships:** People may help themselves to very tiny amounts of food or say they don't want certain things, yet will eat more quantity and more types of food if it is placed on the plate.We don't want to stuff people up with food, but we do want to be as encouraging as we can, short of nagging. While not forcing people to eat, we need to be inventive in exploring what they will actually consume because their brain limitations may be distorting their judgment. So, it never hurts to serve up the food, because they might want to eat it. Let them decide what to do.

5. **The dying do not want to eat:** While there may be varying schools of thought on this, hospice studies and current medical studies show that the body has no hunger and food intake is

more and more reduced in those who are dying or approaching the time of dying.

If a hospice assessment has been made that someone is probably in the dying process, most authorities agree that it is inhumane and unnecessary to try to force-feed the dying. Unpleasant rejection processes are activated by so doing.

Expert guidance from those who understand palliative care best is needed under such circumstances. Don't be afraid that you are "starving" someone who is dying by not making them eat food. You won't be able to and they will vomit or have diarrhea in response to forced feeding.

Duke University School of Medicine carried out studies into the use of feeding tubes and found that they caused considerable discomfort and did not extend life in dementia.

62

Typical statistics also show that about 19 percent of tubes are incorrectly inserted, causing pain and even death because of the procedure. Plus, people with dementia are extremely likely to try to pull out the tube—a sure sign that it feels uncomfortable—and end up having their hands and arms tied down.

Most families worried about feeding an elder who doesn't want to eat would be helped very much by talking with a hospice social worker or nurse. If you worry about these issues, please check into website information on these issues by googling, for example, eating and end of life issues.

Get familiar with what the dying process is actually like for an old ill person. I can tell you, it's usually a peaceful process in which food preparation does not feature very much. It's usually people who know nothing about the normal old-age dying process who worry about that. So don't be afraid to find out more. It'll probably put your heart at ease.

**6. Why People with Dementia Eat So Much Sugar:**  Studies have shown that the brain coping with the destructive physical processes of dementia needs huge amounts of calories.

Plus, the brain itself needs three different kinds of sugars even to work normally, let alone when under siege by a deterioration process such as dementia.

So, this struggle to obtain the nutritional elements needed is often expressed in immense sugar hunger and a huge willingness to take that sugar in ice-cream and cookies. This doesn't work, since those are the wrong sugars and the body dumps them fast into the blood supply and not send them on up to the brain.

Brain sugar is drawn from carbohydrates, so that is where you start battling the passion for ice-cream. And you certainly might want to get those digestive enzymes into people with dementia, since that also supports the process of full digestion. Getting the process of digestion improved leads to more of the essential glucose going into memory function and that's what you want.

However, the body itself clearly demands whatever it can get to try to meet the hunger levels for sugar. Hence, the ice-cream bars and the cookies.

Therefore, added supervision is needed to prevent sugar-binging. Either lock the freezer or remove that ice-cream or buy it only in small quantities or numbers. That's all up to the care-giver.

Don't even think you could train your person NOT to go for the ice-cream. After all, did that work for you? And you don't have the excuse of dementia, right?

## Notes to Self

## WHAT CAN'T DEMENTIA DO?

In one of my caregiver workshops, I try to teach people the magic mantra of caring for a person with dementia. You might find my mantra useful too. It goes like this.

You breathe deeply when annoyed by something your Mom, Dad or Hubby did and you say to yourself, "It's because they have dementia." Here's how the mantra works. Someone says, "I just don't understand why my mother asks me the same thing over and over again."

I make my magic mantra signal and we all chorus, "Because she has dementia!"

Someone else says, "I tell my husband every day to stop answering the telephone."

"And why does her husband still keep answering the telephone?" I ask the group.

Bless their lovely hearts, they all chorus again, "Because he has dementia!"

Do I do this kind of thing just to add to the moments of misery that may occur in a caregiver day? Well, that is part of the fun for me, of course. But mainly, it's to get over to caregivers that many dementia behaviors are simply impersonal.

People with dementia do not do things just to make us crazy. Mainly—yes, go on, say it: "It's because they have dementia!"

So, just to keep things simple, the next section contains a standard list of probable usual failures in people with dementia. Everyone varies somewhat, because people are people. No-one is just their disease.

However, there are issues common to most dementias. So, here's a list:

## What Dementia Can't Do

### 1. Dementia Can't Remember:

Pretty much never in the short-term, dubious for the last few weeks, years or decades, and variable in possibility for long-term. This means you can pretty much depend on your Mom for **not** turning off the stove after you told her 33 times this morning to make sure she did turn it off. Or your husband for not knowing where the coffee mugs are, even though you've told him. Often.

### 2. Dementia Can't Learn:

That's why your Dad still can't make the new remote work — and never will be able to. Get him the simplest one with the fewest buttons. If you can't find that simple one, use what you have but tape over all the controls you don't want him to use. That works pretty well since people with dementia tend to mess less with devices and are usually incurious about what they have there.

### 3. Dementia Can't Plan:

Planning needs reliable short-term memory, ability to think and retain step-by-step ideas and keeping timing in mind. So, NO, your mother did not do that thing to make you crazy.

And let's repeat our mantra here, shall we? No-one with dementia does foolish or annoying things specially to ruin your day. It's important for your own good state of calm to really work on accepting that, otherwise you've just taken on battling with dementia itself. And that will wear you down and kill you, because dementia will win over the battling caregiver every time.

Don't think you have a duty to fight anyone else's dementia. It's an illness. Medical science, doctors and immune systems might fight it. You—not. Admit you're angry, frightened and grieving. Go to a support group, share with your friends, see a therapist or your minister and let all that stuff go.

Instead of fueling your own anger and resentment, breathe

deeply and murmur calmly, "It's because she has dementia."

**4. Dementia Can't Reason:**

You can never win an argument with people with dementia? Why? Mantra, please: "Because they have dementia."

An argument is a step-by-step series of statements made in rational progression, so you can prove you're right and your mother is wrong. Since your mother can't follow the step-by-step thing—"Because she has dementia"—she experiences being confused, attacked and often frightened by you. Therefore, she gets stubborn. That's what fearful people do when they feel attacked. They dig in their toes and refuse to move or they get aggressive in attitude.

Remember that fear and uncertainty are the two dominant emotions in dementia. To make life easier, especially for you, try never to evoke them.

If you think carefully about it—and I hope you will—you can see that making a case in argument needs a temporary short-term memory structure. Your central statement, your back-up and explanations, your demands and requirements.

Nicely-reasoned and well-constructed as this may be—it cannot be held in the mind of someone whose short-term memory function is seriously damaged. That person **can't** do what you want. You may feel the right word is **won't**, but that is because you are angry and frustrated.

Blaming a person with dementia for not doing memory-based tasks is like beating a man with no legs for not running faster. Instead of being angry, either make the right moves to take care of things or admit you're looking to be angry at your person.

If that's the real truth, I'll bet you're over-tired, over-worked, feeling trapped and probably grieving and frightened too. So, the truth is that you need to make a care plan for you. That should be your real priority. And look at the last point below.

**5. Dementia Can't Win:**

And it's true. People with dementia can't win any more.

That's what we caregivers most need to remember. People with dementia have lost the life they once had. Only you as a caregiver can bring something else to fill that loss.

Dementia **can** laugh, enjoy, have fun, be absurd, act lovingly, be kind, enjoy the cat, but only if you can let go of the things that make you unhappy, over-tired, resentful, afraid. Because one unhappy caregiver can make life hell for the person trapped in dementia. And, really, it doesn't have to be that way.

Do you know why? Because you **don't** have dementia. You **do** have choices. People live more happily with kind caregivers. Dementia does better in a non-dramatic, non-accusing, non-angry atmosphere. So, if you are so exhausted and over-whelmed that you behave verbally abusively, you are in serious need of a break. Perhaps you need a permanent break from caregiving and there's nothing wrong with that.

As someone who has worked with other people's families extensively, I have to say that quite often family care is actually not the best care for a person. Because you love your mother doesn't necessarily mean you'll remain the best caregiver for her. Long-term caregiving is a task different from most others.

It doesn't have vacations, nights out and time off, unless you organize that. If you cannot get that relief, then it would be better to find a good care home for your person. There are plenty of good ones out there, too. Places where your person would be better cared for than you can manage.

Think of it as sharing the care, leaving them the daily 24-routine and you the special times. You can also use them for respite help, for yourself. If you want a vacation—and, please, do want one, okay?—then find a pleasant home-like small place you feel you can trust, and take your vacation.

As a caregiver, working way beyond your energy level and feeling total loss of control is not admirable. It's terrible. Because, while you may feel like a prisoner, there is only actually one who is a prisoner and you know who that is.

So be kind to yourself. Be clear about the help you need and the time off you must have and get organized. It really will be worth it.

## *Notes to Self*

## MAKING SENSE OF DEMENTIA

It's true there's lot of mis-communication going on in dementia. You're  going out with friends and you tell your Mom,
"Now, Mom, whatever you do, don't turn the light off, okay?"

You get back home and have to stumble around in the dark
and then you get in an argument with your Mom. The latest of
many since you took over her care. Well, that's because you don't
really take it in what having dementia means.

I can give you some handy guidelines which might help. These
are my "**Let's not get crazy**" reminders abut dementia. They include you accepting that **short-term memory problems** means
a person can't remember an agreement, a discussion, what was
said and, for that matter, what has been forgotten.   So there's
no point in you going on about it, okay?

So, you're annoyed. Well, I certainly understand that. Why not
take your annoyance into a room by yourself, write the name of
the annoying person on a piece of paper, place the paper carefully on the floor, then jump up and down on it. There, that's
better, isn't it?

Having dementia also means being unable to argue back. If
someone does try to argue—you for example— you'll get stubborn
or angry and your person may get agitated or even cry. That's
because having dementia  means you often feel lost, lonely and
frightened.

Having dementia means someone can want  Mom so badly
they don't even remember she died forty years back. They'll sit
and cry right now for her to walk back into the room.

So, a lot is lost. But here's what's not lost. A person doesn't

69

lose life experiences, though those might get lost inside sometimes and not be easily evoked. Even when they are lost within, they still happened. That's because life events are experiential, not intellectual.

Intellectual people hardly ever understand this and they often regard a person with dementia as empty because intellectual capacity may be seriously damaged by dementia.. But everything done, seen and felt is still somewhere there within. The life formerly lived does not un-happen.

The right moment or right person may evoke that life again. So, caregivers and visitors, always assume that a person is still fully a person. It's just the front brain system functions which are lost. A person does not lose their own feelings.

In fact, those feelings often becomes a major form of communication. Unfortunately, a caregiver not in touch with personal feelings, may well have no idea what someone else wants, needs or is truly saying by showing feelings.

Many people with dementia actually become much more feeling that they've ever been before. They are in touch with their emotions and their emotional responses to the outer world and to their inner memories. That's what happens when right brain begins to step in and take over lost left brain functions.

Feeling memories finally emerge, having often been hidden away for a long time. That's why you'll find a man finally weeping for his little brother's death, a woman admitting her childhood sexual abuse at last.

Just be a sympathetic listener and say, "I'm so sorry." If your person seems better and more relaxed after this outpouring, then this is healthy grieving. Support it. Don't try to fix anything, because you can't undo the past. But you can honor it.

In dementia, needs are not lost. Unfortunately, former ability to express them is often broken. A caregiver has to try to understand what's going on. So, when an old man asks if Mom is coming home to dinner, a good caregiver understands intuitively that this person needs mothering.

Some deal with their own uneasiness in the presenceof dementia,
by devaluing that person. They may choose to see dementia as
signaling that someone is empty, gone away, brain-damaged
and therefore valueless.

That is a terrible fate for someone who is often becoming
much more feeling-based and whose feelings have become a
valuable form of communication.

All humans seek emotional comfort, resolution of emotional wounding and the experience of unconditional love. It is the
heart of the human journey. People with dementia are always
on that sacred human journey. The terrible thing that happens
too often in our society is that people are encouraged to discount
the one with dementia. There is a terrible bigotry about it.

This is the worst thing that happens in dementia. It is worse
than having dementia. Much worse than having dementia is
having a caregiver who has all those judgments.

Unable to interact warmly and caringly, such caregivers 71
create enormous anxiety and fear in those they care for. That is
one of greatest factors in acting-out behaviors in people with
dementia. We don't do much harm by just not being sure what
to do. And we certainly don't do harm by being kind. So, if your
person is upset or unable to express something clearly, you can
do great good by sitting and being there, even if inside you're
thinking, "What the heck do I do now?"

## Notes to Self

## THE SECRET DEMENTIA

It is obvious to me, from everything I have now experienced in my 20 years of dementia care, that dementia starts at least 20 years before anyone outside the experience notices.

Maybe longer. Maybe it really is some genetic tendency you're born with that just takes a long time, or the necessary triggers, to make it develop. Like arthritis. Or heart disease. Or after-effects of a head wound. That I don't know and I do hope that medical science will be able to tell us perhaps more clearly how it happens, as research continues.

But I do know that dementia takes time to develop. Especially in the years just before it begins to outwardly manifest. People experience its encroachment into their lives and are aware of this, though they might not say anything to anyone about it.

People might experience any of the following signs of possible dementia. They may have periods of memory loss which may feel like a sense of absence. This can be the loss of recall that they're describing, unfamiliar with what it really means;
There can be a loss of cognitive ability for a period of time, perhaps fairly short in the beginning, but recurring and perhaps becoming longer. One woman, in her 40s, described to me her experience of getting into her car and looking down at the gas and brake pedals, suddenly aware that she had no idea what to do. She consciously made herself relax, with slow breathing, and gradually the knowledge returned.

She had this same experience in other situations and had already had an MRI done by a doctor who had suspected she might have a brain tumor but failed to find anything to account

72

for her lapses in cognition.

Some people feel attacks of extreme fear , due to the inner knowing that something was badly wrong. These can manifest outwardly as inexplicable attacks of rage or sudden and unusual episodes of heavy drinking. Other forms of emotional outbreaks can happen.

These might be sudden weeping, loss of emotional control, or even wild accusations of a kind that might sound paranoid but are actually extreme fear reactions. This might include stories of neighbors stealing, people breaking in or strangers in public places may seem menacing. Clearly this is a symptom which could apply to a number of mental health issues as well, so it needs in-depth investigation, as does everything else in this list. As so often in dementia, behaviors or reactions might be clear, but the reasons for them are not. Any group of these signs occurring mean, "Get me to a doctor—something's wrong."

Stories of losing the car, getting lost on the way home, of having a wallet stolen and other. incidents that that don't quite make sense begin to accumulate, even though you don't know what to make of them. You don't have to be able to diagnose anything, just to notice that things are changing and the reason is not apparent.

Few people are both willing and able to share their sense of disquiet with family members, but some do. One woman, who had been dealing with an increasing sense of incapacity to carry on as before, said to hr husband one day, "I don't know what's going on, but there's something very wrong with me. I just can't do the things I used to any more. You're going to have to."

After medical investigation, she was diagnosed as having a dementia of the Alzheimer's type. And her husband did indeed begin to take over the tasks that had once been hers.

Their situation was unusual in that she was very open and honest. Even though everyone knows about Alzheimer's dementia now, people are still seldom that honest with each other.

## Speaking Dementia

Denial is still the most usual thing that happens. People
are so fearful and think it so awful they don't want to be around it.
It is confused with all kinds of things that aren't even related
-- severe mental illness, PTSD, brain injury issues. Maybe
we could all start to think about how we need to
change all that and have it be just one more illness that we
could learn how to deal with.

### Notes to Self

_____

## WHEN DEMENTIA IS INVISIBLE:

Most people think dementia starts when you see it. You know, with memory glitches that are consistent, serious and obvious to everyone. With being unable to run daily life. Not keeping things going the way you used to.

Everyone knows that these could be pointers to dementia—although we'd also be smart to realize it could also be due to many other possible illnesses or issues. Very many of these illnesses and conditions manifest the way we think dementia does.

But what goes on in that time period in which there may be NO outer manifestation of dementia and yet the individual concerned knows there is something wrong? We don't hear much about that stage, the time which I call the **Invisible Dementia.**

How do I even know there is an Invisible Stage, since by the name alone it's—well—invisible? I know because of documentation that I noted in three separate people that I cared for. To those early observations, I've now added twenty more years of watching and adding many stories from caregiver families.

One woman was a 79-year-old German Jewish refugee in Berkeley. Hannah, who had won her college degree at 64 but at 74 had been diagnosed as having Alzheimer's. She was the first person I had ever looked after with Alzheimer's and I was very curious about the whole development of the condition—as I still am.

Hannah had kept voluminous diaries all her life and her family agreed to let me read them as a way of knowing who she once had been. I was also, however, looking for clues.

75

I felt sure this was not a disease that started only when others could see it. That didn't make sense to me at all. I found that first clue in the diary she kept after her husband's death.

She was about 50 at the time he died. I found a passage in which she talked of "this terrible absent-mindedness of mine." It was the first mention of anything that might be construed as the beginnings of dementia.

This was 24 years before her diagnosis. Later on, her diaries much more clearly showed her issues of short-term memory affliction that we are all familiar with in dementia. But her first reference was subtle and unusual —an "absence" was how she described it.

A second example came from the life of Sheila Moon, a famed Jungian analyst, poet and writer immersed in Navajo culture. She had become profoundly affected by dementia by the time I met her. She had been diagnosed as having Alzheimer's, although her medical history included an episode of mercury poisoning much earlier in her life.

I also found out in my next two caregiving decades that an unusually large percentage of people with dementia had a very difficult childhood, as did Sheila herself. Following my work with Sheila, I was able to see dementia as also a journey in which people might at last receive what they never had. Unconditional love and care. Mothering.

I have always been grateful that Sheila Moon in her own illness became one of my great teachers. She also talked in a "word salad" style, fluently and easily chatting along in a nearly incomprehensible mix of words apparently pouring out at random from her inner brain dictionary.

This is now considered to be an indicator of frontotemporal lobe dementia (FLD). Sheila was diagnosed, in the 1980s.

Then, doctors were throwing the term Alzheimer's disease around freely as a blanket to cover all kinds of dementia and even non-specific or undiagnosed mental illnesses. Which still goes on, by the way.

In spite of her "word salad" symptoms, the longer I knew Sheila, the more I could discern a strong kernel of sense within the chatter. Often, it became clear that she was struggling to express important thoughts about what she was going through. It was Sheila who described her dementia as a journey.

Gradually, from being with her as her caregiver, I came to understand that having dementia in fact was often a journey from the mind to the heart. She herself was struggling to explain the ways in which she felt herself to have grown, in spite of the difficulties of dementia.

In search of clues, I looked through her published books. In "Dreams of A Woman", a dream journal she kept for years, I found references from a particular time period in which she had two important dreams. In one, she was told by a doctor that she had an irreversible brain disease. In another, she met a spiritual figure in a long white robe.

He said she would be asked to join a special order in which she would be of the world but not in the world. That's one of the best definitions of dementia I've ever read, by the way. At the time at which she had those dreams, Sheila Moon was in her early forties.

She would not be diagnosed with dementia, whether of the Alzheimer's type or any other dementia, until her early 70s.

The third clue came from Rebecca. She had run the hospital social work department of a large Bay Area hospital. Retiring at 65, she was diagnosed with Alzheimer's in her 80s. After her death, I helped clear out her apartment. I found, in her underwear drawer, an old folder.

It held a collection of newspaper clippings. All the articles in it were about memory problems. They dated back to her forties.

I understood just by those three examples that dementia began growing inside a person's awareness decades before it ever showed on the outside.

Think of that long loneliness.

## *Notes to Self*

———————————————

## WHAT'S IT LIKE TO HAVE DEMENTIA?

If you have a parent or a spouse with dementia, you probably wonder what people inside the disease feel. If you work in a care facility, you probably also wonder if people know there is something wrong and how they feel about it. One thing that's always okay is to ask them.

Dementia can be a very isolating condition. It can deeply affect how well people communicate. Of course, as we all know, it certainly affects memory. It can be hard for people to even find the words or hold the thoughts they have. It makes it very hard to follow through a whole explanation about anything.

Besides which, it's hard to explain the experience of having dementia. It's a complicated condition with many aspects to it. And, amazingly enough—or sadly—hardly anyone wants to know.

You won't hurt a person with dementia by asking what you want to know. In fact, it might help them feel less lonely. Because of their condition, they might not be able to find the exact answer you want. But that's okay. Listen carefully with your heart and you will find that even trying is good enough for both of you feel closer.

Be tactful and apply what you already know about this person. If it's your Dad, who tries to cover up his problems all the time, you might decide it's sensible NOT to use the word dementia, but just kindly ask how things are going.

If it's your husband, who is very straightforward about his condition, you can talk much more intimately. Be smart and always use discernment. Remember that someone's denial is fear.

79

We don't help people's fear by insisting on lecturing them about their dementia failings. Don't make your person uncomfortable.

**1. Does it hurt to have dementia:** Dementia is not usually a physically painful condition. It is emotionally painful, of course. For family and for the person who has it. If you know someone with dementia who is also having head pains or other physical pain in other parts of the body, they need medical checkups. It is essential to get them to a doctor for help and relief of their pain and possibly for a better diagnosis.

For example, some people diagnosed carelessly as having dementia, actually have cancer, the effects of which is causing the memory and thinking issues that someone thought was dementia.

**2. What do people with dementia think about?**

Having dementia can make clear and flowing thought processes difficult. It is hard to be logical and rational with dementia because brain deterioration blocks the channels for clear thought.

That said, they think about their past, their family, their wants, their needs and maybe sometimes nothing much at all.

They might be thinking about their dog and living at home with Mom and Pappy and enjoying the thought so intensely that it seems they really are still living there. I call that experiencing Deep Memory and it's not craziness. It's the side effect of short-term loss and it's very logical, within the framework of dementia.

They might be thinking about going for a walk. They might have half a thought that drifts away before the rest can be formulated. Or, you could ask. As in, "My, you look deep in thought. What's on your mind?"

**3. Do they lose all memory?**

Not necessarily. Studies show that, while short-term memory becomes catastrophically bad, long-term memory may be anything from surprisingly good to very mediocre.

So a person who doesn't remember anything about this morning may be able to tell you in detail all about being young and living with their parents. It's not quite right to regard them as losing their memories.

It's more accurate to understand that the usual easy brain access to memory is damaged. Therefore, the memories still live within. In various ways or on particular occasions they may be evoked. One old lady I knew had been a piano player for silent films in the 1930s. She no longer had access to the memory of that. She didn't recall that job. She didn't even remember she could play the piano.

However, if you led her to a piano—she protesting all the way that she couldn't play it and didn't know how—sat her down on the piano stool and guided her hands to the keys, she just started right up and could play for a couple of hours.

So, you see, not all memory is locked away in the brain. It is also stored elsewhere in the body. In hands, feet, other parts of the body, stored in actions and stance and activities. All over the body there are those memory boxes holding bits of the past.

### 4. What does it feel like to have dementia?

From my experience, I'd say it feels frightening, lonely, confusing and full of bewilderment. But also, dementia folks feel loving, angry, sad, anxious, grateful and happy, joyful, proud of themselves and able to have fun. So much of that depends on us.

### 5. How can I help?

Use patience, love, tolerance, understanding. And honesty. The best thing you can do is to be the nice version of yourself and also truthful.

You can say things like, "I hate this illness you have!"

You won't hurt a person with dementia by being honest about how you feel. In fact, it might help a lot. It might bring you closer together. Because what you feel about their illness might well be just what they feel.

# Speaking Dementia

Remember, people with dementia are ill, but not necessarily fragile and breakable. So you can talk to them as if they could understand an adult conversation. You'll soon find out if they understand or not. If they don't understand today, they may understand tomorrow.

---

## Dementia and Hallucination

Elders, with dementia and without, experience visits from dead relatives.

According to who you listen to, this is hallucination, a spiritual experience, wishful thinking, imagination or "What the @#%* do we know?" Just understand that such visitations are known to everyone who works in the Hospice movement and they don't think it's weird, so you needn't either. It doesn't need medicating.

In our society right now, there is no consensus on any spiritual or psychological phenomenon, so don't worry. However, you may assume this is not appropriately classified as hallucination. Maybe we could reliably call it an Altered State phenomenon. I think of these as "around-death experiences."

Many other so-called hallucinations may be misperceptions in seeing and hearing common to elders, especially elders with dementia. Seeing poorly and not hearing well are why people hear odd things said and see odd sights. Hence, your near-blind grandmother's alleged "bear in the garden" sightings. So, cut them some slack, okay, before you label them crazy.

Most of the elders I have known who allegedly had dementia AND hallucinations were people who turned out to have serious mental illness. With two big exceptions.

People who have Lewy Body dementia often have interesting hallucinations involving color and unexpected appearances. For example, a friend of mine reports her grandmother used to see colored rabbits playing in her kitchen.

They were purple and and pink and she knew they were not real. "I know they're not really there, honey," she said, "But oh, I so enjoy them!"

Other people experience these Lewy Body hallucinations as frightening. In such cases, I would wonder if there were PTSD (Post Traumatic Stress Disorder) complications in that person's life.

In one of my support group meetings, a wife reported that her husband had recently been seeing little green men out in the cactus beyond their property. He was aware that it was odd to see them and he was amused by his experience. Even more oddly, two months later, a different couple came to a meeting and again it was the husband who was seeing little green men out in the desert. I was intrigued to find out that both couples lived in the same part of town. Go figure that one out!

The other class of hallucinations belong to the PTSD group in the dementia population. Those suffering from PTSD combined with  dementia may experience flashbacks to unresolved experiences. A woman may hide from her abusive father, a man from the invading army forces of Nazi Germany.

Although PTSD is a psychological ailment, it is also a useful reminder that an experience remains to be emotionally dealt with. That is one reason for the flashbacks. They speak to the sufferer of pain and fear not yet processed sufficiently to allow resolution. As caregivers, we can be there to support our person while they share their experiences—possibly over and over again. Even hundreds of times.

So that you don't pass out with boredom, ask questions, walk deeply with them into the dark memories. It helps. You don't have to fix them. You can't. But you can be their witness, companion and protector while they heal themselves.

When is that task done? When they stop talking about it compulsively. Don't hesitate to get more help for them if they need it. If their intensity of feeling scares you, then seek psychiatric help. Good medications may support them better while they do their inner work.

I would informally estimate that as many as 20 percent of elders said to have dementia are actually seriously mentally ill. Never put yourself in danger with the person you care for, nor let them hit you, choke you or even verbally abuse you.

If they seem out of control, call 911. If they seem regularly overwrought, call a psychiatrist and make an appointment for the two of you. Before the appointment, list the behavior you've seen, not your own opinions or feelings. Try to get that list to the psychiatrist before your appointment.

If you feel your person would refuse to see a psychiatrist, then don't tell in advance. Just go for that drive, get to the office and, if your person says anything, just play it down.

You could say something like "Oh, he's going to figure out whether you can get better medicines than the ones you have."

I don't believe in lying, but evasion is acceptable.

85

If you're a paid caregiver and this person is violent, call 911. Too often, seriously mentally ill elders are left unhelped, because their family is in denial. Maybe that family genuinely does not recognize the issue. Maybe they're afraid or ashamed, but no caregiver should be endangered doing the job of caring.

## Notes to Self

## NORMAL WEIRD DEMENTIA STUFF

Since people are so confused about dementia, I'm going to list things that may look odd but are the normal things of dementia.

### 1. Noun Loss

Noun loss is normal. It's normal for people with dementia to be unable to bring your name to mind. It doesn't mean they hate you. It means they have dementia, which is a physical deterioration of the brain, especially in the short-term memory storage areas.

This noun loss may extend to being unable to identify the cat as a cat, for example. Again, due to brain affliction, in some people the connection between noun and object may be lost. So, you could say, "Mom, would you please put the light on?" and Mom may not know what the word "light" connects with.

So she doesn't put the light on. Because she didn't understand you. Try pointing at the object next time when you speak. That kind of cuing often works.

### 2. Calendar Loss

Then there's calender loss. I know you think you came into the world knowing the day, date, time and year, but you didn't. You learned that. In dementia, people unlearn that. They live in the year they think they're in. And that will often be the year they emotionally need to be in. Probably childhood or youth. Maybe later. Eventually, they may permanently move into that long-ago time in which the work of true memory resolution has to happen. Back with Mom and Pappy on the family farm in South Dakota.

86

When that happens, your present name will disappear and you'll get the name of the family member you most look like or whose role you now have.

That's when you become Violet, the name of Mom's youngest sister who died when she was 20 and whom she dearly loved. You are Mom's sister because Mom is now emotionally living in her own twenties again —normal for dementia. And maybe you do look like Violet.

Or she might start calling you Mom, because you are now in fact playing the role of her mother. Or your Dad might call you Mom, as might your husband with dementia. Because you are now in some sense the mother to these people. Instead of feeling bereft that they no longer know you, understand them. They know you're close, you're family, you matter. Relax and forgive them their illness.

### 2. Making Up Stories

Then there's what doctors love to call confabulation and what irritated family members sometimes call telling lies. I call it staying sane. Seriously, you try living in a world where you can't recall yesterday or who these people are around you or your daily routine.

I see the stories people tell as setting a fence of sanity around themselves, to reduce the stress of all that loss. I enjoy it. It's a healthy survival mechanism. The less a person has in their life, the more extravagant the stories they invent. In care facilities, old ladies will tell you they were married seven times and had 21 children, even though they were married once and have one daughter who never visits.

Listen and learn and enjoy. Comfort. Don't judge.

### 3. Wandering

Everyone knows about the wandering issue in dementia.You and I call this walking and we can do it any darn time we choose. Your Aunt Esther in the Memory Care facility is called a wanderer because there they don't even have a safely enclosed walking path.

87

Wandering is what people with dementia do to self-medicate their anxiety and stress. They may also be in search of the way out of the building. Or maybe it's a more metaphorical journey in search of time past.

Whichever applies, a wander needs a walking program. Someone has to organize that for them. You know who that's likely to be, don't you?

4. Eating weird.

Now your Mom only wants to eat candy, ice-cream, cake and cookies. She needs supervision. Maybe also to have digestive enzymes, to enable her food to send those vitally-needed sugars to the brain. None of those brain sugars are to be found in ice-cream or cookies—wouldn't you just know it?

Mom doesn't want her green food to touch her yellow food. If you want her to eat—and you do—you'll just pay attention to what she wants. Don't argue, just do it, Missy, okay?

88

Try small meals often. Make the food bright, small, interesting and tasty. Step up the flavor a lot because she is losing the ability to taste and smell food. Try smoothies, sweet fresh fruit with little chunks of cheese, things she can eat with her fingers. Not all food has to be eaten at the table—and, by the way, do you sit down and eat with her? Because you should.

Sit together on the sofa and eat finger food while you watch reruns of Oprah.

Frena Gray-Davidson

*Learning To Live Dementia*

## LEARNING TO SPEAK DEMENTIA

All your first lessons in speaking dementia involve you saying nothing, okay?

Why would I tell you that?

Because all human communication is based upon at least 35 percent body language—and sometimes 100 percent. That driver whose truck you just rear-ended and who's marching towards you, fist-clenched and jaw tight? Nothing said, but 100 percent you know you're in big trouble, right?

That's body language talking to you. And we speak body all the time. Think about it. That snooty woman you don't like on sight, before she's said a word. The whispery timid person who makes you afraid to speak to him in case you scare him even more. The disapproving old lady who looks as if there's nothing she's liked since 1937 —you aren't rushing over to sit next to her, are you? Body language. Eloquent, to the point, says a lot—without a word.

And body language says even more to the average person with dementia. Why, dementia makes you so smart that you know when your own daughter is angry at you, while she has no idea how angry she is. With dementia, you can read people's anger, fear, unhappiness and agitation, while they think you know nothing about how they feel. So, don't say a word until you've learned how normal dementia works.

### Normal Dementia

The first noticeable thing that happens to you in normal dementia is that gradually you lose the ability to access your short-term memory. You know this long before anyone else notices.

That's because it's a long slow process. By the time others notice, you have probably been unable to retain short-term memories for some years.

Having short-term memory damage means you don't remember yesterday at all. You may not even remember five minutes ago. You well may have forgotten or become unclear about the last ten years. That's pretty frightening for anyone. It makes you feel unsafe, insecure, alone.

You may react to these feelings in different ways. Some are angry and fearful, others depressed. Some withdraw from human contact. These are all emotional reactions to the terror that memory damage causes inside you.

As if that weren't bad enough, growing damage to the part of your brain that does cognitive thinking also begins to affect you too. It's not that you're becoming stupid. Or that your I.Q. has diminished. It's that you can't retain the steps in thinking things through. You can't do rational thinking process reliably any more.

Before you were ill, your wife would say, "Honey, I need to write a check for $500 for the property taxes before the end of the month or we'll be in trouble," and you heard, remembered and understood everything she said.

Once the damage to your brain affects the once-easy flow of thought information, your wife's sentence might be heard in this way. "Honey, I need [forgotten] $500 for the [forgotten] or we'll be in trouble."

Aware that you don't understand, you react angrily to what you think was said.

"I'm not made of money. You're always spending. I'm not giving you anything,!" you shout. And you refuse to hand over the checkbook.

Your wife weeps, you rage and neither of you know that this is part of the language of dementia. The process of not-understanding in dementia is as eloquent as understanding is between those who don't have dementia.

This is the very beginning step in learning to speak dementia. We who care for people with dementia need to develop a deeply compassionate sense of empathy for people whose very brains are betraying them.

We need to understand the terror, confusion and desolation that can sweep over them every time they are reminded they can't remember stuff and every time they hear information or questions they just can't understand or answer.

Imagine it. Maybe you're pretty bad at math. A rotten cook. Lousy at the computer. But you can remember your day and your yesterday. You can retain a whole sentence in your memory in a conversation. You're able to take part in social life.

Now imagine this. You're a Nobel Prize Winner. Or you ran the Opera House of a glittering world-renowned city. Maybe you're a famous film star, a writer, a poet. You can't remember what someone just said to you. And you have no idea who they are.

Once you have dementia, all the things that once were part of your very structure are no longer there for you. You may forget your whole last twenty years, including all your attainments.

You have lost your operating power, because memory, intellectual organization and remembered life experience give that to you. Even driving the car is a challenge. And dementia takes so much of normal life away.

When we caregivers understand that, we begin to learn to speak dementia. Before we ever say a word, we have to understand the losses that people with dementia are forced to live with, every day. Then we have to step up beside them, in honest admiration of how they manage. Not with useless pity.

We walk with them on their day's journey, so they can be more. Because we speak dementia so tactfully, with true compassion, we add warmth and comfort to a frightening universe. Without learning these, we never create care which helps people with dementia to feel safe with us.

When we don't do that, we set ourselves up for all kinds of difficulties, from behavior problems to fear-related violence. And it's our fault. People with dementia can be demanding in their care needs, but they are seldom violent unless they feel threatened. When we haven't learned dementia basics, they do feel threatened.

**Top 10 Dementia Basics**
1. People with dementia **forget** a lot;
2. Because they forget a lot, they feel **afraid**;
3. Because they're afraid, we must **slow down**;
4. **Arguing** doesn't work with dementia;
5. **Logic** doesn't work;
6. **Bossing** people around doesn't work;
7. **Kindness** works;
8. **Humor** works;
9. **Heart** connection works;
10. **Persuasion and suggestion** work.

Often, we caregivers get into trouble with our people who have dementia because we misjudge what dementia is all about. However, it's very important that we take into account what dementia is like for the person who has it. That helps us to remember **how we need to be** for successful care interventions with them. We have to move into their world of being and start there, learning them all over again. Because dementia changes them.

**Important facts About Dementia:**
1. People with dementia are **NOT crazy.** Short-term memory loss means starting each day anew.

2. When people with dementia like you, they feel they know you, even if you just met. **Kindness helps** create this trust and trust helps eliminate difficult behaviors.

3. No-one becomes a non-person just because she has dementia. People just lose **reliable access** to their former life.

Everything they were is still somewhere within. Maybe they can reach it sometimes. Often, a good caregiver who gets to know their person well can evoke who they were.

An old woman, who has forgotten she used to play piano, might play once her hands touch the piano keys. It's only her head that's forgotten. Her hands can still play. A dancer has feet that can still dance. It's our job to help find out what remains accessible.

As caregivers, we can often help replace empty space in a dementia life with old joys. The woman who can no longer make quilts might love to color patterns. Doing that is likely to bring the same calm and achievement she used to know in making quilts..

People with dementia do things oddly, because they forget the steps in-between that make life work. As caregivers, we can help fill in those in-between steps for them. Then they can do something or enjoy something that brings them comfort.

**94**

Very often, their level of emotional ease depends very much on how we care for them. Our bad day can be hell for them. Our little meanness takes all chance of love that day away from someone whose only hope of love we are.

I'm sure you don't neglect or abuse whoever you look after. But do you fully face your responsibility to be the bearer of love? Do you act with respect? Are you kind?

If you're not, because you had a fight with your husband or your teenage daughter, then the person you look after will pay for your bad mood all day long.

The best thing we can do, quite often, is to stop pretending. Your people are your prisoners. That's the truth. So, please, leave your troubles on the doorstep. And free them into that kingdom of love with your heart.

Remember that all of learning to Speak Dementia begins with the silence of sitting within yourself while you open your heart to understanding.

## CAREGIVER BODY LANGUAGE

Before you can really be a great caregiver, you need the right stance for the job. Since people with dementia are sensitive, frightened and often confused, your body language must say, "I come in peace."

How do you say that with your body? Pretty easy, actually. Take a few deep breaths so you can tell where your tension is being held. Then consciously relax those areas. If you're a typical caregiver, you probably have only breathed between your throat and your shoulders for a long time now.

Tension and worry does that to us. That means, your poor body is oxygen- starved and your shoulders muscles clenched.

A good breath goes gently from nose all the way down to below your belly. Take a few long gentle breaths. Not big steam-engine breaths, just long and slow and soft breathing. Then think a beautiful thought. Did I hear you just snort with derision, Missy? I thought so. Poor baby.

Let's try that thought thing again, shall we? Just remind yourself that today you will find at least one thing to enjoy. A bird in the yard. A cloud in the sky. Your lunch. The peace when your Mom is snoozing on the couch.

Find one thing to enjoy. Once you do that, then try to find one thing an hour to enjoy. If it helps, write a little list of anything you find to enjoy.

Don't tell me you can't enjoy until this ordeal is over. That's one of the big lies overwhelmed caregivers tell themselves. In every day, no matter how hard, you can choose to let go of the negative. You do it by taking little baby steps. One tiny step out of your locked-in fear, tension, anger, exhaustion.

We humans can choose to seek greater happiness, to have a moment of peace, to let go of our negative thoughts and attitudes.

And, believe me on this, if you go into a room as a resentful, angry, weary caregiver, your person picks that up immediately. So cut it out. Moment by moment, one breath at a time.

### Non-Threatening Body Language

1. **Be at the same level**, sitting beside them or sit on a chair at about the same height. Or, kneel beside them so they can look down at you. That's very safe and people with dementia never think it's weird.

2. **Never loom over** people with dementia. It's impolite and is usually perceived as threatening. If there is no chair for you to sit at the same level, then **kneel.** If you can't kneel, go find **a chair.** When speaking, keep your voice calm. A loud voice, even when meant to be friendly, may not feel friendly to a person with dementia.;

3. **Use reassuring touch.** While talking, touch the person's arm or hand in a light friendly way. This helps most people feel relaxed and more in contact. If you feel a movement away, remove your hand immediately;

4. **Speak more slowly** and simply, so you present one idea at a time. Don't talk down, just be more simple. Move slowly. Touch gently. Think kindly. This signals to the person that everything is okay.

5. **Respect space.** Give the amount of space that seems to meet this person's needs. Near enough or far enough. If someone is angry, step back to give this space. Never step forward into someone's anger space.

Frena Gray-Davidson

*Notes to Self*

———————————————————

## UNDERSTAND DEMENTIA DEEPLY.

For me, one of the most profound and wonderful processes we witness in dementia is the deep inner journey towards finding peace.

Yet, it is also often totally misunderstood, misinterpreted or — amazingly—not even noticed by family and caregivers.So, let's all notice from now on. Let's speak out. Let's watch out for these examples of the process at work.

We caregivers have to become our own researchers. Then we have to teach others. People with dementia do not have to continue being regarded as empty gone-away people who need something like rabbit care. We need to ask ourselves, what it is that is going on in our people with dementia?

Supposing it's your Mom. She doesn't seem to be very present at all. She is absent, as if absorbed somewhere else. Is this just emptiness, dementia or what? Well, brainwave activity studies confirms that plenty is going on in there.

This person really is absorbed somewhere else. Usually childhood or youth, in the parental home. So, here you are. Arizona, 2012. Your Mom, also Arizona 2012, to all appearances. In reality, however, inside her memory, she's living in 1926, South Dakota, with Mama and Daddy. She's ten years old.

You panic and think, "She's deluded, hallucinating."

Calm down and ask yourself how could a person with short-term memory issues have this day, date and time right anyway?

Before we make judgments about what we're seeing, we need to learn what real dementia looks like. We need to think how being memory stricken actually affects someone.

Just as a legless man can't run, a person with dementia can't remember normal daily stuff any more. That includes not be-ing linked to a day/date/year calender within. That's a short-term memory task. And it's gone. And they've moved to long-term memory territory, because that's not gone. That resides in a different part of the brain.

So, what exactly ARE our elders with dementia doing there in the Land of Long-Ago? They are doing the **Great Life Review**, silly. They're examining life with Mama and Daddy. Re-living, re-experiencing, re-examining, making sense of all that happened.

Why would they feel they really were there? Two reasons. One, short-term memory loss. Two, the intensity of their memory experiences making an intense re-creation of a distant moment.

You probably never read about this anywhere else, as far as I can find out. So pay attention. Almost everyone experiences a deep intensification of memory, starting in the late 50s and deepening as they age. That is what allows the deep healing which results from their memory work.

We know about this phenomenon from trauma. Trauma creates flashback moments. But flashback is not necessarily only associated with trauma. It has powerful healing possibili-ties. Flashback experience happens in order to remind us to revisit that which requires our attention. When we give it our attention, we open the door to healing.

People overwhelmed with trauma experience this. Flashback is merely intensification from memory which asks for our attention. That is why elders working on the understanding of their lives experience that same intensification.

And it is also why our old people with dementia experience it. Because they have lives too. And their lives ask for that same deep attention so few of us give our lives until we reach old age.

In therapy, maybe we do it. In creativity, almost surely. In old age— absolutely. In old age, **with or without dementia**, elders do the **Great Life Review**. That's why our elders with dementia seem absorbed and far away sometimes. They have just been dwelling in the very distant past. Welcome them back respectfully. Ask questions. We have had so little respect for people with dementia, alas, that we have not even considered asking them about their own thoughts, feelings or wishes.

But we could say, "You seemed very far away just now. Where were you?"

You might get some wonderful answers.

## *Notes to Self*

## How Dementia Works On Memory

Dementia often comes about through physical deterioration of the brain. Certain areas are especially targeted and peo ple lose abilities controlled by those areas.

The most obvious is the ability to remember in the short-term. The phrase "short-term memory loss" is not as exact or universal in meaning as you might hope. It has a variable meaning, according to each individual affected by it.

Short-term might be a few minutes, a few days, a few months, a few years or many years. Each individual is affected somewhat differently. One person might forget the answer to a question, then ask it again. Most people forget yesterday, but might remember a special yesterday. A visit from someone beloved. A new pet maybe.

The eventual range of short-term memory loss might extend for years. One woman forgot the whole marriage to her second husband. She only remembered her first.

Memories are embedded not only in the brain computer, but also in emotional impact. Whether wonderful or terrible.

One woman recalls clearly the joyful birth of her first baby. Another woman reacts fearfully as if her father were still around to abuse her. A man recalls his little brother drowning in front of him. These are memories embedded by emotional impact.

Family members may feel memory loss as an emotional rejection. As in, "My father doesn't even know me." Actually, their father may well emotionally "know" but is prevented by dementia from getting the right noun out.

The whole emotional and psychological shaping of human life tends to be that early life makes the biggest impact, for good or bad. That memory is laid down so deep that little can displace it, other than major brain injury. That is also why an elder is drawn back to that early deep territory—parents, home, belonging, fear or joy. Both elders with dementia and elders with great memory and excellent health are drawn to spend a lot of time in that territory.

It's not useless dwelling on the past, as uncomprehending people sometimes think. It is the great coming to terms with what happened in a life and how we transcend pain, make sense of people, confront our losses and turn our minds to the divine. It is the great life review.

And if we all did that before extreme old age, we wouldn't make so many damaging mistakes in our lives. Better late than never, though. To me, the fascinating aspect of that great memory work is that people with dementia also do it.

They do it differently, cause they have dementia, but they do it. You've heard them, but maybe you've dismissed it. You didn't know what you heard. You heard an old woman, a demented old man, talk about living back on the prairie. About Mama and Father. About people dying of scarlet fever.

That was it. The great work of memory, done even in dementia. I don't know about you, but that makes me feel humble that the soul always does its journey.

## Notes to Self

---

## TYPICAL HOUSEHOLD DEMENTIA ISSUES

**Phone:**
Don't want hubby to answer the phone while you're out? Then turn the ringer off, turn down the sound and let voice-mail pick up. Also give out a cell-phone number for important business calls;

**Boredom?**
Involve your person in the daily tasks you do and lower your standards, so what they do as acceptable. It's entertainment, not hotel standards. Explore going to a day-care program

**Need time out?**
Organize a same-sex expedition of some kind—fishing for hubby, shopping for wife. If that would work for them. If it was successful, try it again. Why same-sex? Assuming that it would be more relaxing, since obviously a stressed-out you can't be relaxing for them.

You can use your time-out for any of the following—a long soak in hot scented bath (well, that's my favorite choice), a nap, a movie, walk with the dog, meal with a friend or even therapy. Whatever calms you down and helps you out of your state of stress. Wanting to train people with dementia is usually a clear symptom of being highly stressed.

# Speaking Dementia

# I

Frena Gray-Davidson

## WHERE DOES MEMORY LIVE?

Memory is not just a brain thing. Triggers which stimulate brain memory into activity are to be found all over the body. Even in the brain, different areas of the brain are associated with different kinds of memory.

For example, the short-term memory function is considered to be largely centered in the frontal lobe area of the brain. However, the brain process is a whole chain of linked functions. The eye sees, the brain interprets, the person thinks. In dementia, we are working with a person who is unable to think as before. That complex chain of connection has become fractured by the physical wounding to the brain structure. The following is my inexpert summary of brain geography.

**Frontal Lobe**

This sits behind your forehead, approximately, and has many very important functions, affected by dementia. It controls overall thinking and is an area associated with the rational activities of organizing, planning and problem solving, as well as processing of short-term memory. Dementia may cause any of the following:

1. Inability to remember what was said;
2. Inability to follow an argument;
3. Inability to think rationally;
4. Over-sensitive to perceived attack;
5. Easily provoked to anger or tears.

These may translate into daily problems with remembering, decision making and normal routines.

### Parietal Lobe

This can be found behind the frontal lobe. It processes and stores the integration of infomation from the five senses of **smell, taste, touch, sight and hearing.**

This information gives us guidance and help in decision-making. Burning food smell would normally warn us to switch off the stove burner or oven.

However, the person with dementia is unable to process the information being transmitted by the burning food. No alarm is created and therefore no response comes about. That's why people with dementia can't cook safely.

### Occipital lobe

Found at the back of the brain, is a vision control center. The information received by this vision center is then processed by other parts of the brain, responsible for decision-making, response to information and carrying out a plan. As in, making a plan to sit centered safely on the toilet seat. Something most people don't think twice about, so automatic are our reflexes.

Dementia damage done to various parts of the brain may make interpretation impossible. Successful interpretation is based on accumulated past memory and experience.

Without reliable access to memory and brain function, the shadow of a tree branch may become interpreted as a bear in the back yard. This is not hallucination. It is the result of being unable to interpret information accurately. In other words, if you don't live in bear country, the average person doesn't think of bears in the yard. The person with dementia, however, is unable to stay anchored to normal life and any thought might occur and stick, regardless of accuracy.

### Temporal lobe

Near frontal and parietal lobes, this is communication central for smell, taste, and sound. It also has responsibility for the formation and storage of memories. This is one of the most terribly-wounded parts of the brain in dementia.

When ravaged by dementia, it cannot begin the formation and storage of memory any more.

We who don't have dementia never think about how our own memory works. We mainly assume something happened and we remembered it. However, the process is much more complicated than that—wouldn't you know it?

When something happens, the brain immediately begins to activate a chain of command which will take that happening in our mind from short-term memory and place it into longterm memory storage. It's like taking something from your own house to put in into your storage unit across town. Brain experts say it takes about two hours for a memory to move from short-term memory to long-term memory storage.

The brain of a person damaged by dementia is unable to carry this through. So, even if something happened only yesterday, it's gone. It left short-term memory and didn't arrive in long-term memory. Gone.

This leaves a person at the mercy of fairly random information retrieval. This starts to fragment a lot of aspects of memory. Not just what happened, but how to do things, what to decide, how to behave. Even, sometimes, how to dress, what bodily feelings mean, how to understand what people are saying.

When someone helps, there may be a moment at which knowledge comes flooding back. A vocal cue or the familiarity of the movement itself—any of these may remind the person. I learned this from Hannah, the first person I ever looked after who had dementia.

She'd forget how clothes went on, but she'd dress anyway. Then we'd tussle with her sweater, to get it off her foot, on her arm.

"Ah, now I remember!" she'd cry out in triumph halfway through the process and she'd complete her own dressing successfully. Her body reminded her, apparently.

For family caregivers, the struggle is to truly understand that their person is not doing things to be annoying or resistant. **They cannot help what they cannot do.**

As their caregivers, we have to work on our own stress tendencies which trigger our anger or blame response to their wounds of function.

## *Notes to Self*

### Learning to Handle Dementia Behaviors

People with dementia are often feeling frightened and
alone, even when they're right there with you

I wonder sometimes if having dementia is like one of those
UFO stories. There you are, minding your own business, living
your life. Then one day, or so it might seem, you are trans-
ported away to another planet where no-one is familiar and the
life you knew has gone.

That's how I think of it. They are taken to **Planet Dementia.** No
wonder they're scared. And sometimes angry. And often lonely.
So as a caregiver, I try to bridge that gap. Every day I introduce
myself, again. I'm not willing to test their memory and watch
them fail.

It's so easy to say, "Hi Mom! It's me, Mary. "

It helps and it's never wrong. If Mom does recognize you,
she might say something like, "Of course I know who you are,
silly!" It just saves a little extra stress. And that's always our
hope.

**Bathing:**

If I'm going to help someone to bathe, I'll do it something
like this. "Oh Mom, let's get your shower done now. You'll feel
so great afterwards. It'll shake the ache out of your muscles."

Say it your own way. Just don't ask the direct question, "Would
you like to have your shower now, Mom?" She might say no.
Develop major essential caregiver skills in **Suggestion, Bribery**
and **Manipulation**. And I mean all those in a good way.

If my powers of persuasion fail, signalled maybe by Mom bashing me with the back scrubber, I'll back off.

I'll **apologize,** "Oh I'm sorry, Mom, I didn't mean to scare you," and I'll help her feel safe before I try it again. These apologies apply even more to professional caregivers.

And maybe sometimes I just have to leave the shower out entirely that day, though usually not. By the way, daily showers are not good for the compromised skin of elders. Maybe three times a week, maximum. Otherwise, the old-timey washcloth and water in the basin trick is fine

When you want **compliance,** say, "Fred, why don't we...?"

and

"Mary, let's go and..."

and

"Mildred, I bet you'd feel better if we..."

People with dementia feel secure with suggestions. If they already feel unsafe, paying no attention to their wishes is a sure way to terrify. If we respect and respond kindly, trust is much more likely to happen. Here's some guidelines.

**The Rules of Handling People with Dementia:**

1 **Don't worry them;**

2 **Don't hurry them;**

3 **Don't hesitate to "Sorry!" them**

4 **f they get mad, step back;**

5 **If they feel sad, step forward;**

6 **f you frighten them, apologize;**

7 **Never argue - no-one wins;**

8 **Never order them about.**

When doing care tasks, ask "Would it be okay for me to...?" and "Do you mind if I...?"

Every time you ask, you empower the person with dementia. You give respect. You build trust. Fear levels reduce.

Most of these rules apply just as much to your own family

111

members as to taking care of others professionally. There isn't one courtesy for strangers and none for your own. Never make assumptions about familiarity with your family member who has dementia. Dementia can put a lot of strangeness into daily life and routine.

Remember, **caregiving is the building of relationship**, not doing a bunch of tasks. The person with dementia may well have a seriously damaged memory. The heart, the spirit and the soul within, however, are fully alive. Nurture them.

Become a companion.

## Notes to Self
_____

## SUCCESSFUL DEMENTIA INTERVENTIONS

If an emergency intervention needs to happen in dementia, it often requires action which is the opposite of what you might think. Dementia normal is not ordinary life normal.

That, by the way, is exactly why care staff and family caregivers walk, or even run, right into trouble sometimes.

I'm not talking medical emergency, but behavioral emergency. When things heat up in dementia, we usually need to slow down and often to step back. That is an appropriate response to one person being upset in a dementia situation.

**Behavior emergencies in dementia care**

1 **Anger** in response to a frightening situation—such as bathing or simple confusion;

2 **Agitation and upset** in response to a distressing situation, such as a family member trying to show you where you went wrong in what you did;

3 **Resistance and anger** in response to being ordered about;

4 **Stress** in response to be being hurried;

5 **Hitting out** in response to frightening invasion of space. We should know the person we care for We should know what upsets them. If we know what upsets them, we should modify our behavior. Amazingly enough, people still continue to do what is known to upset a person. Perhaps lack of training, sometimes thoughtlessness. Sometimes due to anger on the part of the caregiver, or a dominance attitude

113

A resentful internal voice saying: "Why should I give him what he wants?"

Or, as expressed to me once in a care institution where we were considering a care plan, "But, if we always give her what she wants, won't she just get spoiled?"

That resident. by the way, had only been there about four days. Scary, isn't it, that making an effort to reduce stress and displacement trauma in an elder could be construed as "spoiling" that resident.

But it is quite frequent that care staff may have punitive inner mothers, usually for the simple reason they had punitive outer mothers. Care staff brought up with dominance and power in the home need  guidance towards the power of love as a management tool. Eventually they may come to enjoy it, because force uses up so much personal energy, and they may really embrace the chance to feel at peace.

114

Frankly,  most of us mess this up  sometimes. We tend to mishandle situations when we are tired, lonely, fatigued. So, even if we are those things, we need to step back into that part of ourselves that allows us to still be in kindness mode.

Staff and family caregivers both need to develop the ability to quickly contact their own sense of nurturing. That guides us all into more intuitive and helpful action in situations.

We can very usefully approach difficulties with apology, as in the following situations.

"I'm sorry, George, is it okay if I give you a hand here ? I know your arthritis makes it hard for  you to shower easily";

To a resident getting angry, "How about you and I go for a walk and leave these folks behind?"

To a woman crying because she wants to go home, "I'm so sorry, Mildred, I know you really miss your family at this time of day. Shall we  talk together?"

I won't say kindness always works, but it always work better than anything that doesn't include it.

## WHY ARE PEOPLE WITH DEMENTIA SO DIFFICULT?

Good question! Well, why are they so difficult, those people with dementia we care for? Our Mom, Grandma, that old lady in room 13? After all, we mean well, don't we? We're the good guys, the ones taking care of them. So, why aren't they more helpful, less cranky?

There, there, sit down and take a nice deep slow breath. Very good—now take nine more. Here's the thing. Think of it like this. Having dementia is like talking English in Italy.

Dementia is a different language which is hard for caregivers to learn well. Because deep down inside we often think that, at any minute, this person will return to normal again. But they can't. They would if they could.

**Where Do Caregivers Go Wrong?**

1 **We refuse to learn and respect normal dementia;**
2 **We fail to empathize;**
3 **We resist the changes of dementia;**
4 **We argue, rather than adapt;**
5 **We give orders and we seem unloving;**
6 **We resist necessary change.**

The normal signs of dementia include **memory** problems, difficulty with **logic**, emotional **neediness**, **loss** of skills. These are all usual and seldom improve. Yet, many caregivers try hard to make people relearn how to do these things properly. This creates frustration and anger in the caregiver and fear and frustration in the person with dementia.

Overwhelmed caregivers can easily turn into blamers. They blame people with dementia for what they can no longer do.
This may be understandable longing to have back the one who used to be. However, it creates a climate of fear and anger. It also makes the caregiver's work twice as hard. It is much easier, in fact, to step up beside the person with dementia. To say in your actions, "I'm here. I'll help."

It's easier to equip the house the way it needs to be. Lots of hygiene equipment in the bathroom—undies, vinyl gloves, wipes, garbage bags, masks. Support bars on the wall. Wash cloths, liquid soap dispenser, lots of toilet paper, a good sense of humor. You, only better.

It's easier to accept the changes and learn to communicate and how to get what you need as a caregiver. It's a big energy saver to learn how to persuade your person instead of creating resistance.

116

You'll feel much better if you vow to shut up nagging and sit down beside them and put your arm around them. Be a good companion. Love. Let go. Forgive. If you're resisting all that, look deeply into what's going on with you. Hey, let me give you a clue here—anger, sorrow, fear, loss and grief. That's just for starters. Resentment. Dislike. Revulsion. All common, alas.

Care for yourself first. Then become the caregiver you need to be. When you do that, I promise you that everything will change. You'll be able to learn your person as this person-with-dementia. Which often has its own peculiar charms.

For sure, you'll both laugh more. You'll be on the same side. And you, the caregiver, will find this is a deep soul journey of the heart, like no other. Plus, everything you learn and every strength you gain will never be wasted in the rest of your life. It's all useful stuff.

## WHY DO PEOPLE WITH DEMENTIA MAKE YOU CRAZY?

Your Aunt Enid is feeding the squirrels under the impression they're pussycats, right? And Uncle Henry isn't much better. He keeps asking you what time his mother is coming to dinner tonight. Uncle Henry is 92, so you know the chances of his Mama coming to dinner are zero.

Sometimes you wonder if you're the crazy one, don't you? Well, perhaps you are—but only because you don't take time off. Here's the deal. If you want to do a good job of caregiving, you must do it right. That means, you must have the following:

**Must-Haves For Caregivers**

1 **Time off;**

2 **A good night's sleep;**

3 **Social time** with someone who doesn't have dementia;

4 **Understanding of dementia,** such as knowing you can't train your person;

5 **Discipline** to fill your caregiver life with your own activities as well.

Many of the things that make caregivers feel crazy are simply the ordinary daily life things of dementia. If you're willing to let go of your rigidity, you'll do better. Normal dementia behaviors include **forgetting. Repetition. Actions** repeated over and over, which is also because of forgetting.

So, if it's making you crazy, that's a sure sign you need a good night's sleep or time out.

Just to remind you, yet again, here's the list of things people with dementia can't do. It's typical that they **can't remember short-term** things, which extends anywhere from 5 minutes ago to 20 years. They also **can't learn new tricks** nor re-learn old tricks now forgotten. They **can't do step-by-step rational** thinking.

However, the things people with dementia **can do** include being able to **eat well, laugh, love, sleep, enjoy music,** love their pets and follow their own personal delights.

So, yes, they will make you crazy if you're requiring them to remember things, give in to your arguments and do what they used to be able to do.

And I'll be saying that again because the most difficult thing for caregivers is often simple acceptance of where a person with dementia is at in the disease. **We are powerless over dementia.** We do have to let go and let dementia. So go ahead and put that burden down.

118

If you're interested and ready for an easier time, here's how not to be crazy. Get a good night's sleep. Plan your time off. Get respite helpers. Go to a support group. Be loving (because you hate yourself when you get mad at them, right?). Practice forgiveness of yourself and your person. Have fun. Have more fun. Have too much fun.

It's important to really learn what goes on in dementia. Many people don't. Then they get mad about normal dementia behaviors.

S upport groups help you understand everything better. Read good books on dementia—cheerful, practical, up beat books, like mine. Never read a book that is all about despair. That won't help a bit.

One thing I always love about people with dementia is they aren't very judgmental. so you can be your own self. If you're grumpy, they forgive you by forgetting. They don't mind if you're wild and crazy, within reason.

Actually they usually enjoy it. And it helps you have playtime in your working day.

So, get back in there and waltz that darn cat until somebody laughs. And what a lovely gift that would be for the both of you to enjoy.

### Notes to Self

## Calming Dementia Down

Your Mom has dementia. Every afternoon, she gets really up-set and agitated for a while. That upsets you. Now there are two of you, upset and agitated.

A friend tells you she got her Mom tranquillized with medica-tion prescribed by the doctor. You're reluctant about using heavy meds. Is there an alternative?

The answer is YES. However, first you must be very sure what you're actually dealing with. It's essential to have a full Alzheimer's work-up done on your Mom.

You really do want to find out if she has some fixable, adjustable, other medical condition going on. That is what the Alzheimer's work-up is all about, to find what can be fixed.

Is there such a thing as normal dementia? Well, after 20 years of caregiving people with dementia, with alleged demen-tia and with probably-not-really-dementia-at-all dementia, I'd say there is normal dementia. Everyone does dementia in his or her own way, because everyone is an individual.

**Not Normal Dementia**

**1. Person is rage-filled much of the time;**

**2. Is spontaneously violent;**

**3. Rampages round the house all night long;**

**4. Hides in closets, terrified;**

**5. Believes attackers are coming to the house.**

This is not normal dementia. Such behaviors indicate the need for investigation of possible serious mental illness, or PTSD.

Wild out-of-control behavior is not usual in dementia. These folks need expert psychiatric help. Some people have struggled with the deeply wounding after-effects of war trauma, childhood abuse and other traumatic events that have caused deep and lasting stress which we call PTSD. These folks too need the intervention of skilled psychiatric expertise.

Such elders may all be able to still continue living at home once they are receiving the kind of expert help and medication that their condition requires. Indeed, such medication may bring them the first real peace they've ever experienced since their traumas.

So, let's assume you know your parent is not dealing with such issues, but is really only struggling with what we'll call normal dementia. That can be handled.

Normal dementia agitation is often called **Sundowning**, because typically it tends to happen towards the end of daylight. To help, you stay calm and breath deep and slow. Remind yourself that agitation doesn't actually harm a person. It's just upsetting. Once it's over, only you remember it.

"I know it's upsetting (or scary, or annoying or your choice), but it's going to be okay. I'm here and I won't let anything hurt you," you might say, kindly.

You listen carefully, noting anything which describes feelings of fear, uselessness, abandonment and neediness. You'll find you can probably support the reality of that feeling with kind words.

"I know you really miss your Mom. Come and sit here and let's figure things out together."

Remember, agitation passes. Just stay calm and kind and hold your own center for a period of time. If certain things set it off, make a plan. If it's sundowning— that late afternoon regular agitation event—you make a detailed sundowning activity plan.

That includes nourishment, security, kindness and re-direction, all of which work well.

You hear that everyone with dementia has sundowning, but that is not true. Even in the case of a person who regularly has sundowning, carefully crafted care plans for the individual can reduce and even eliminate that agitation. I have seen this done and I have done it successfully myself. And you can too.

The whole next section is on sundowning, because -- for many people -- it's the hardest part of care. And it's the thing most likely to get an elder subjugated into submission by heavy meds, such as anti-psychotics. That may be appropriate for people who are properly identified as psychotic by psychiatrists, but inappropriately prescribed anti-psychotics injure and kill elders who merely have dementia.

If you really don't know what to do for someone who is undergoing sundowning stress and agitation, it really doesn't hurt them if you do nothing but sit it out. It is a cycle which passes and you can merely be there and be supportive and em-pathetic.

122

## *Notes to Self*

Frena Gray-Davidson

## Dealing With Dementia Tantrums

L et's face it, folks, an awful lot of so-called Alzheimer's violence is not even due to Alzheimer's. Nor to dementia of any
kind. Not that I'm diagnosing here, you understand. I'm just
sharing my observations, in case they prove helpful for someone out there.

So-called Alzheimer's rages might well be a serious previous-
ly-undiagnosed mental illness, such as paranoid schizophrenia.
You think that's incredible? Well, these days, I even recognize the
warning keywords that suggest to me that family members need
to get a psychiatric consultation for their person, as well as an
Alzheimer's work-up.

Examples are "Mom's nerves," "Grandma was difficult,"
"Auntie Em was suspicious of strangers," or "Dad never wanted
to see anyone." So, no, I'm not diagnosing, just suggesting that
family members ask themselves, is there something else going
on there? Schizophrenic and psychotic elders don't belong with
those who have dementia. And they may not belong at home.

Also, seriously-mentally-ill elders deserve to finally get the help
and relief that the right intervention, treatment and medication
can bring to them, sometimes after a lifetime of turmoil and fear.
People with dementia are not intrinsically violent. They are re-
active, not instigators. When people with Alzheimer's have what
I'd call tantrums, we can usually figure out what it's about.

Most are fear-driven. They typically occur through caregiver
error, often involving invasion of privacy. They usually occur in
the bathroom, in connection with bathing or toilet use.

They also occur when a well-meaning caregiver steps forward, instead of back, and invades a safe barrier. Sometimes, they occur when something just too surprising happens.

**The Five Most Common Factors**

1 **Bathing;**
2 **Using the toilet;**
3 **Emotional upset due to family interactions;**
4 **Physical shock;**
5 **Old bad news** forgotten and now repeated, such as a parent being dead.

**Bathing** is often a fear issue between people with dementia and their shower. This can happen at home but it more usual in a care facility. But every home should have that **hand-held shower**. People with dementia hate water beating on their head.

In care facilities, it is the main reason for staff being hit. It comes from speediness and insensitivity from task-driven care staff. Staff need to introduce themselves daily, ask permission to help, start showers with a **hand-held shower** moving up the body from the feet. They also need to respect reluctance when it is manifested.

Every resident in longterm care has the legal right to refuse medications and procedures. That means, staff need great communication skills.

And these same approaches should also be taken by family members. Just because it's your Dad or your spouse does not exclude the possibility of an adverse reaction if your family member becomes frightened or confused.

Going to the toilet is a lifelong private matter from age 5 to the onset of dementia. A caregiver should be relaxed and sensitive. Emotional upset is usually the at-home scenario for dementia tantrum. The spouse, usually a husband, is upset, probably due to fear demonstrated as anger. It's usually closely connected with all the emotional overload of a family dealing with dementia.

Possibly even failing to talk openly about it, a secrecy
which is foolish and misguided because those with dementia
are very aware of emotional undercurrents.

Usually the husband has anger, good wife moves in to
soothe him and **WHAM!** People with dementia need space
when angry. They need you to step back—and apologizing
might help too, okay? Give time for the tantrum to pass and it
will.

Physical surprise is something unpleasant happening suddenly, which brings emotional eruption. A blast of cold wind in
the face—very upsetting for those with dementia. Being rained
on. Walking across a pleasant lawn when the sprinkler comes
on causes, as I witnessed once, shrieks, and wailing.

Hearing bad news can set off an emotional tirade. Your
mother asks where her mother is. This is because, in her normal
dementia, she doesn't know this day, date, place or year. You
kindly tell her that her mother is dead. She reels back in shock
as if hearing it for the first time—which she is, sort of.

Better learn the kind of pleasant cunningly evasive communication that caregivers master. Or maybe an understanding question in return. "You're missing your Mom right now,
aren't you?"

A wise caregiver might does some motherly comforting
things.

*Notes to Self*

125

## AVOIDING DEMENTIA VIOLENCE

We hear about it all the time, don't we? How someone with Alzheimer's hit his wife. How a care facility resident punched a member of staff. Alzheimer's has a bad public rap for violence.

However, speaking as a long-time dementia caregiver in a variety of settings, from at-home to care home and day activity program, a lot of the time we caregivers bring about those episodes. If we learn what makes people with dementia react badly, we can be more careful and kind.

**Five Ways We Upset People With Dementia:**

1 **We forget to ask** nicely if it's okay to help. Instead, we just start invading the person's space without waiting.

2 **We speak and act too fast**, which is upsetting and confusing to someone with dementia.

3 **We give orders** and nobody likes that, okay?

4 **We try to argue** the person into obeying and it's usually impossible for someone with Alzheimer's to follow an argument. So they'll become stubborn and resistant.

5 **We move too close**, when really we should step back and apologize.

Like us, people with dementia prefer to be treated with respect. Like us, they feel safer if we learn what they need. It's easy to stress our people, especially when we caregivers are in a hurry. We need to slow down as caregivers.

**How To Win Co-operation:**
1 Be nice;
2 Use humor;
3 Persuade, encourage and bribe;
4 Be patient;
5 Be kind.

All of the above are very powerful tools in managing good care of a person with dementia. Dementia is not some mysterious, unknowable world beyond. It is a health condition which afflicts memory, cognition and rational thinking.

If we work within its limits, we can make great relationships with people. They need that desperately. Too often, people with dementia are treated like children. But they are adults, doing their best to function, with broken skill levels remaining. Dementia terrifies the people who have it, so we must be reassuring, not hurried, angry and demeaning. Dementia gives people really good emotional radar to know when we're only pretending to be nice.

It's very tiring to have dementia. Ironically, it does not involve having an inactive brain at all. A brain with dementia is constantly in over-drive, even in sleep. Dementia people dream much more than most people. The brain is always struggling endlessly to get through the blockages somehow.

People with dementia often visit other time zones in the past. At those times, you'll very likely be called by the name of someone from that past. The present won't make sense to your person. Just accept it. They'll be back.

People with dementia are adults. Adults with a deteriorating brain, it's true, but their wish is to be helped to live as adults and to be respected. When we violate that wish, and don't respect their losses, we invite responses that we won't like.

127

That might include hitting, which might be our fault. If we are better caregivers, our people are more secure, less fearful.

We really need to admit our own faults and accept people with dementia just as they are. They need our warm and friendly attitudes and for us to take time for our care tasks with them.

It never hurts for you to ask yourself, "What would I like if I were this person?" If nothing else, the questions reminds us that this is a person much like us, only burdened and entrapped by a lonely disease.

A person made, not more simple, but more complex than most of us.

A person who still has many possible ways to find life good. And we caregivers are often the gateway for this to happen.

## *Notes to Self*

*Growing Your Caregiver Heart*

## THE FAMILY CAREGIVER REWARD PLAN BENEFITS

Everyone knows looking after someone with dementia can be very difficult. And it sure is extra helpful if you aren't related to the person.

As an outside caregiver, I've always enjoyed my people with dementia. They had their illness  from the first moment I met them. That was why I was meeting them.

I admire family caregivers so much. I respect and honor what you all do, because you do so much. Often  putting your own job aside to go home to care for Mom or Dad. You  take on something you maybe  never wanted to do. And you've taken on something difficult.

Heck, dementia is so difficult that you could almost count on most of your friends deserting you if you have it. Yet, you family caregivers step in there and you take it on. Even though it can be so scary to look at Dementia Mom or Alzheimer's Dad with the question, "Could this one day be me?"

So, in you go anyway, to  do what no-one else in the family wants to do, though they'll probably have plenty of opinions about how you do it. Even in the family, the family caregiver is not always respected.

Very often, as the family caregiver, you aren't even paid  for what you do. Sometimes you are scarcely thanked. But don't let all that worry you. I promise you, the rewards are great, right here. Right now. Right in your life and continuing to the end. In your life, in your  growth, in your  heart and soul.

You see, all you family caregivers, struggling from day to day, maybe wondering if the light will return to your life, here's the real truth.

You're the person who ultimately will never be afraid of illness, death or dying again. Usually, the caregiver of a person with dementia also becomes a person no longer afraid of dementia. As long as they have grown to understand the inner being of people with dementia. They learn that no-one is ever NOT the person he or she is, in spite of the deep changes illness brings.

As the family caregiver, you grow inner strength to carry you through anything. You know that, while it's not fair that everyone in the family didn't help as they should, it is the caregiver who gets the rewards.

Maybe not material rewards, but the rewards of courage, self-respect, ability to face old age and dying with that reassuring sense of already knowing how all that is. Often, the family caregiver is the one to finally heal from the family wounds, while the others simply don't. You are the one who comes to find out in this illness a person was simply living out whatever his or her own wounding had been. You learn from all of that.

Not many hands-on caregivers still carry resentment, sorrow and inner lack after being with a dying parent through the process. We caregivers learn that life marks people in ways that some choose not to seek healing from, others too broken to do that.

We caregivers know that people's greatest fears emerge when they are dying. We caregivers can see it. When we walk with someone to the very gates of death, we know something deep about living that can never be shaken again. When you've done that with your own parent, you are a spiritual hero.

You will never lose that.

## GOOD CAREGIVER—BAD CAREGIVER: YOUR CHOICE

Okay, so you're your Mom's caregiver. Or your Dad's. Or your Grandma's. And, though you're a bit scared, you're going to do your best. Wonderful! But have you chosen the right best to do? Are your choices even possible? Let's take a look, shall we?

### Fighting Your Mom's Dementia

You can't fight dementia. Leave that to doctors and researchers and drug companies. They have the time, the money and it's what they're supposed to do. There isn't one bit of convincing evidence that shows caregivers can hold back dementia.

132

Best choice is to try to have a good day together. Leave the impossible to others. You can't stop dementia and your job is caregiving.

### Re-training your Mom's memory

Bad choice because, remember, your Mom has dementia . That means she can't remember. It means she does not have the supporting brain cell structure now to remember. Trying to make her remember is like trying to make a paralyzed man walk. Not very possible and not too kind.

Good Choice would be to leave that to divine intervention and modern medical science and, meanwhile, try to have a relaxed and pleasant day.

### Taking your Mom to see old friends again.

Hmm. Maybe good, but often not. People with dementia often withdraw more from social life and it usually isn't because they are depressed from isolation.It's because they are so overwhelmed by too many people at once.

There can be too much talking with too little ability to understand everything. So the planned enjoyment is actually upsetting.

And, sad to say, often those old friends don't quite know how to be with your Mom as a changed person with dementia, the disease most feared by most older Americans.

Try it by all means, but if it doesn't work, don't push it. It's not like taking your little one to daycare.He has brain power to grow on, your Mom doesn't.

However, you could look for a good day activity program especially for people with dementia. That might turn out to be a great comfort for your Mom.

**You orient your Mom to time, day, date, year and place**
Good luck on that, but here's how that often works—if Mom doesn't FEEL that it is today, this year, this place, you are unlikely to be able to persuade her. More likely, you might puzzle, upset and bewilder her.

Just let go of that. It's not as important as you think. What is important is that you create a day that is enjoyable, easy and stress-free for your Mom, whatever its name, date and year may be.

Like you, I wanted to save people I cared about from their disease. Today, I can tell you, I probably just made them miserable. I didn't realize that at first. It took me a considerable time to let go of my ambitions on their behalf and settle for just a more enjoyable day.

Eventually I lowered my expectations and I raised our joy factor tremendously. And if right now you don't value the joy factor, maybe you're like I was.

Relax. It will take all your time to learn typical dementia, reduce stress., find fun things to do and to keep your Mom involved in daily life tasks together with you.

You see, if you aren't having any fun, I guarantee your Mom is not. So ask yourself from time to time: Am I having fun yet? If you aren't, do something about that.

## *Notes to Self*

## Fixing Mom's Dementia

**I**f you really want to fix Mom's dementia, a really skilled diagnosis is what you need. Because, the right workup may reveal that your Mom does not have dementia at all. What else looks like dementia? A lot of things, actually. That's because, what most people think of as dementia, often is not. We amateurs notice some memory loss issues and a bit of confusion, and we decide, "This person has dementia."

However, we're often wrong. There could be something quite different going on.

**What Else Looks Like Dementia?**

1. **Too much medication** of the wrong kind;

2. **Too many medications** mixing inside the one person . These can cause the appearance of dementia. Be especially suspicious if a new medication preceded the dementia signs;

3. **Physical problems** can make people seem confused and out of touch with reality, including reduced sight and hearing ability. This may well confuse and isolate elders.

4. **Actual illness conditions**, such as getting insufficient oxygen to the brain may be causing temporary and fixable dementia.

5. **Other hidden physical problems** that result in dementia, such as having a cancerous tumor growing somewhere in the body, dealing with serious liver conditions, having heart problems, or a series of mini-strokes leading to dementia.

6. **A hospital stay** often causes temporary dementia in an elder, more accurately called delirium, a state which may well pass once the person is back home. It usually takes a few weeks for

the confusion to pass. This all-too-common condition is due to unfamiliar and stressful environment, isolation from normal human contact, over-medication with new drugs, bad food, too little sleep and constant noise and light intrusion throughout the night.

7. **Dehydration** increases or even causes the appearance of dementia at home. Elders have a very reduced thirst response and therefore do not recognize that they need fluids. Older people commonly do not drink much water. This results in most of their fluids being coffee, tea and soda drinks. Filling a water jug and setting a small glass beside it, with instructions to drink it all by the end of the day may help. Tell them the doctor gave instructions for this.

8. **Other common causes** of dementia as a new issue include having had open-heart surgery, which saves lives but also results in cognitive damage in 33 percent of all patients.

136

9. **Severe vitamin deficiency** is not uncommon in elders with limited diet who never get any sunshine and possibly also have a history of excessive alcohol consumption.

10. **The longterm use of drugs** meant for short term use, such as anti-anxiety drugs, can also play a part in the development of dementia.

This complexity of issues is exactly why it is very important to make sure someone does the full Alzheimer's work-up. Medicare pays for it and it is extensive—MRI; CT scan; blood, liver and oxygen testing; extended social and medical history taken; brain pressure test and the whole works.

That little mini-mental test doctors do in the office is not a dementia test. It just indicates memory issues. The full Alzheimer's work-up needs to follow.

The Alzheimer's work-up is really to find actual provable medical conditions. When everything findable has been eliminated, then a diagnosis of "dementia of the Alzheimer's type" is the diagnosis. That means, looks like Alzheimer's.

Dementia is a more accurate description until and unless medical science actually finds the definitive chemical, gene or symptom that says absolutely that someone has Alzheimer's.

Dementia is a more accurate word because, **while all Alzheimer's is dementia, by no means all dementia is Alzheimer's.**

So, if they diagnose your Mom as having dementia, can you fix that? Maybe not, but you can create care around her that helps her do better. Maybe some of the memory drugs can help, though none cure, yet. Be open to trying them, but note any negative changes in your person and also keep up on reported side effects by looking on the internet. If a medication makes your person worse in any way—from balance to diarrhea to eating—report back to the doctor and don't be afraid to refuse the medication on your person's behalf.

If your Mom's been living lonely and afraid, then care and company could help a lot. Eating poorly? A better diet really can help. Too little water definitely increases dementia, so increased water can help.

You learning to be a better caregiver can help a lot too. Learn the handling skills for good dementia communication—no arguing, no ordering about, take time, be kind, keep it simple. I've had more interest and fun in the last 20 years with people with dementia than probably you can imagine right now.

Relax. Breathe deep. Forgive a lot. Cultivate your sense of humor. Pray. Get enough sleep—see, you're having more fun already, aren't you?

## Notes to Self
_____

## What Stresses Dementia Caregivers Most?

Recent studies on care workers caring for people with dementia reveal that their greatest source of stress is also what stresses family caregivers most. It is the problems with communication.

Family caregivers report this as their greatest challenge also. We can all understand that, can't we? Mom is changed by her dementia and we don't know this version of Mom. We have no shorthand for this Mom. We don't know what she means when she can't say what she means.

It's frustrating. Scary. Time-consuming, Unrewarding. Oh yes, and stressful. Very stressful.

I'm an outsider in all of this. I've never had a family member with dementia. It was cancer, heart attacks and industrial lung diseases that demolished my family members. So, right now, you're thinking, "So, what does she know about what we go through?"

I've had over 20 years of watching families and caregivers and people with dementia go through their stuff. I've been a hands-on dementia caregiver for two decades. Out of what I've seen and tried, I've been able to help people with dementia become much more calm, to reduce their sundowning or even have it stop altogether, to help their fear and agitation go away.

And it's not due to my advanced medical background, because I don't have one. The one thing I saw immediately the first time

I ever cared for a person with Alzheimer's was that this person did make sense.

That wasn't what her sons thought. They were as enraged, frightened, blaming and lost as any suffering family. But, because she wasn't my mother, I could just get on with learning who she was in dementia, right there, right then. And so could you.

It's easy.

Not the loss and mourning part. That's yours to carry to resolution. The easy part is learning Dementia Mom. You can reduce your dementia stress when dealing with Mom or Dad, or spouse, by growing your ability to listen, breathe peacefully; be in that person's present moment (which could be 1927, but so what?).

Additionally, it would help if you were also slow to move, kind in speech and were willing to ask questions and figure out what the answers mean. In other words, learn dementia. Most caregivers are stressed because they try to fight dementia itself. They want people to get their skills back. They want to train them to do better. They want them to remember what they were told. They want to win arguments with them.

Well, dear caregivers, you can't have that with dementia. You just can't. When it comes to dementia, you can't stop it, you can't change it. You can't win arguments, you can't re-train someone and you can't have them back just as they were. Not yet, anyway and that could change literally at any minute, depending upon medical research.

Choose to be with them, on their side in their now, then you have them close again.

It's not the stuff to do that hurts so much. It's your unwillingness to step into the present moment with who this person now is. That's what creates 90 percent of the caregiver stress we hear about—the other ten percent is the endless amount of stuff to deal with.

I invite you into whatever now your own family member is in

139

so you stand beside them. Oddly enough, you'll find you both feel better.

## *Notes to Self*

———————————————

## Companionate Care in Dementia

It's what I call Companionate Care and it's the best kind of caregiving for someone with dementia. It's a relational, friendly, non-blaming care in which caregiver and companion hang out together, doing stuff, not doing it, whatever.

The advantages of the Companionate Care approach are that it reduces anxiety and fear, creates a feeling of safety and offers security It creates a sense of belonging. It's more fun for everyone.

It often takes a little while for the new caregiver to learn to be a companion to someone with dementia. Dementia, after all, changes people. We first need to take some time to learn all over again who this person is now.

It's not that the original person is entirely gone—not at all, though you may think so at first. It is more that the original person is disabled in a major way. We have to learn what that means and how to help. And, at the same time, we may be learning who we are as caregivers.

Which brings me to the kind of caregiver I pray not to have if ever I have dementia. I call this kind of caregiver, the Oppositional Caregiver. These are the ones who have the most terrible things to say about dementia and they very seldom recognize their own part in creating those difficulties.

The problems with Oppositional Caregivers are that they want to re-train the person with dementia, therefore creating an unending arc of stress. They ignore whatever remains whole, thus denying valuable ways to make contact.

They are often anger-driven through stress. They blame the person for the illness and also feel guilty for blaming. Finally, they concentrate on lost abilities and not on remaining capacities.

These attitudes, which are usually fear-derived rather than innate meanness, lead to unwholesome caregiving in which they stand over those they care for and demean them. They try to hurry people, even though those with dementia need time to process information. They take a blaming stance on repetition, sundowning and other complex behaviors, instead of simply recognizing that these are normal in dementia.

They tend to strongly resist working within the capacity of the person with dementia and easily become stricken with pity, guilt and repulsion, instead of gathering caregiving skills.

From what I've seen of oppositional caregivers, there is often a poisoned river of undealt-with issues running through the family. Plus, a great terror of dementia and of having it that causes enormous inner disquiet.

To be a good caregiver asks of us that we face our own inner issues. Caregiving will always raise them, whatever they are. Just because you come from a troubled family, it does not mean you can't learn to be a great caregiver. In fact, looking at the percentages, I'd guess that such a family is almost a pre-requisite for good caregiving. A very high percentage of professional care staff come from troubled families. In caring for others, we often heal ourselves.

We can all become great Companionate Caregivers by learning dementia, by being honest with ourselves about who we are and being willing to get help, support and therapy if needed. We can develop flexibility, forgive ourselves our imperfections, find fun things to do out of perfectly ordinary joys— making cookies, going for a drive, cutting coupons out of the newspaper.

Most of all, we can stand beside those we care for, nurture that which is still available in them, encourage them to talk about the

Frena Gray-Davidson

long-ago days of youth, appreciate them and be peaceful.

## *Notes to Self*

---

## Dementia Bigots

Times have changed and now we can't publicly parade some of our more unseemly forms of bigotry. Not only is racial and ethnic slurring officially banned now, but we also can't make fun of people's illnesses, infirmities and handicaps. Darn it, eh? Where is the fun in life these days?

Well, you'll be glad to know that, apparently, there is still one target you can hit. You can use any ugly words you care to about Alzheimer's and other dementias, it seems. You can say that people with Alzheimer's are gone away, empty or not at home. You can describe them as vegetables, the living dead. You can complain endlessly about the fact that they can't even remember your name or keeping saying the same thing thirty times over.

At one level, I get it. It's scary when someone you knew before is now a person with dementia. It hurts you when they can't remember your name. You pity them when they can't manage even to dress themselves well any more. You're repulsed that they need help to go to the bathroom.

Many of the things that caregivers or family members complain about are just the normal symptoms of dementia. People repeat themselves because they have wounded short-term memory. They need help because they are ill.

It's not all about you. You, after all, can do many things to help yourself be a better caregiver. A better person, even. You can learn to meditate or go to stress management classes. You can change every aspect of your life. None of that is true any more for a person with dementia.

144

Frena Gray-Davidson

Even difficult behaviors are often manageable, when we learn how to manage them. Sometimes that will indeed mean managing ourselves better.

Sometimes it needs you learning to listen with your heart, instead with your ego. For example, if your Dad calls you by someone else's name, yes, you can get all upset because he doesn't seem to know you. And many people do. Even though they know having dementia means having short-term memory problems, they still choose to concentrate on their own feelings about their own name.

What if you listened deeper? Whose name does your Dad use? Is it your long-ago now-dead aunt's name? Do you know what he's saying then? He's not saying "I forget your name because you've always been a bad daughter and now I can punish you for it. "

If he uses a name from his own long-ago childhood, that is the time zone he's mainly living in now. If he uses that name for you, he is actually saying "I know you, you're family, we're attached." He is actually recognizing the attachment of love. He just can't get the bio-data right. That's illness. It's not a statement about what he feels about you.

I am constantly humbled by the immense effort those with dementia make to still try to reach us out of their state of being kidnaped away by this disease. They're trying all the time to say, "I'm here. Can you hear me? Can you see me?"

If we would grow our own power of forgiveness, then we wouldn't hold their illness against them. And we would recognize their magnificent courage.

Could we all try that more? I guarantee we'd all feel better.

145

## No Psych Speak Here!

As a caregiver of people with dementia, I just hate to hear people applying the language of psychiatry to dementia. It simply serves to create barriers to relationship and understanding. It doesn't help at all. Instead it encourages family members, who may well not understand the differences, to think of their Mom or Dad or Grandpa as being mentally ill.

Given the huge amount of prejudice against the mentally ill in our society, we really don't want to bring that into the way we look at elders with dementia. I blame Hollywood for part of this. Using the words "dementia" and "demented " to describe people wayyyyy out of control has only tended to confuse everyone even more.

Wrong words for dementia are psychiatric words. They belong to the world mental illness.

**Wrong Vocabulary NOT to Use**

**1. Paranoid.** People with dementia are not paranoid. They are scared, because they are losing their short-term memory and can't keep track of life.

You'd feel just the same. Heck, Alzheimer's is the one disease most feared by all Americans, so why wouldn't someone who's actually having it be very frightened. That's really quite sensible. And it's up to caregivers to help calm that fear.

**2. Combative.** People with dementia are not violent because they have dementia. They hit out at you when you are an unskillful, invasive, bossy caregiver who frightened them by your actions.

When you invade their space, some people with dementia will hit out. When you don't ask permission and when you overwhelm them with your own agitation. If you take time, remain calm, treat them with respect and consideration, people with dementia don't hit you.

**3. Perseveration** is the psychiatric term for repeating the same words, phrases or questions, over and over. That's actually not due to anything psychiatric, in dementia. It's due to short-term memory issues and relational or emotional needs which possibly are not being addressed or understood.

"How was work?" repeated several dozen times by your Mom may possibly just be her way of trying to have a conversation with you.

If you'd say more than "Fine!" it's possible she'd feel more connected and less lonely. Then she might not need to keep repeating her question. It always worth asking yourself, what does a question really mean in dementia speak.

Someone who asks over and over "Where's Mama?"—when Mama died well over 50 years ago—is trying to signal to you that he or she really needs the kind of loving care that ideally a mother would give. Probably that person also feels alone and-scared. Respond to those needs and the question will probably go away.

**4. Delusional** is a term very often just plain wrongly-used in dementia and it is used as blame-indicator to make people with dementia wrong and ourselves right.

In dementia, two unsual memory issues may come together. One is short-term memory losses, which means a person is no longer able to retain memory of the present day. Two is the normal old-age memory intensification of long-ago experiences. This is why Grandpa thinks he's going to school tomorrow. That is memory wounding, not psychiatric illness.

147

The issue of whether people with dementia have hallucinations is a complex one. If it's dead people coming to visit, sorry, but that's a normal part of old age and dying life. It's very rude to classify a universal phenomenon found in every culture as mental illness in one of them. Who's to say the dead can't visit? Certainly not a psychiatrist of no faith at all. In hospice work, the visits of the dead to living are recognized as very comforting and not otherwise classified.

As someone who works with the dying, I never even try to classify the around death visitation scenarios. In our society now, we don't even have a vocabulary adequate for it. However, such visitations could be imagination, projected emotional longing, actual visits by the spirits of the dead or phenomenon produced by the chemical brain changes in dying. No-one definitely knows and, moreover, it does matter because it's not our experience. It's the personal interior experience of the one who is approaching dying.

The universal characteristic of these experiences are that they are very comforting and very real to the dying person. That's good enough. Let them experience that without outsiders — that's you—having judgments.

If it's other things, like purple bunnies in the kitchen, it may well be a bye-product of the actual dementia type that a person has. For example, Lewy Body Dementia people do have hallucinations, and they usually state that they know they are just seeing things. In other words, they are not fooled by their very real hallucinations into thinking they are real.

If a person with dementia regularly experiences hallucinations which are extended and involving, it's very possible that these are other conditions which do require a psychiatric intervention and diagnosis. Typically, PTSD may be the issue, either from military and battle experiences or from childhood sexual abuse, and other extended trauma situations.

A person can also have both dementia and a psychiatric condition, which is termed a dual-diagnosis. In such cases, that person may well have the delusions of mental illness, as well as the mis-interpretations of dementia.

If someone newly experiences hallucinations after a change of medication, it is appropriate to guess that the medication is the problem. Contact the doctor, google the medication name plus "side effects" to find out the experiences of others. Ask the doctor to prescribe a different medication with the same helping capacities.

Let me just remind you WHY we should not easily allow the language of psychiatry into the world of dementia. Because it tends to nullify communication between the person with dementia and their caregivers, if caregivers are led to believe that dementia communication has no worth.

Caregivers who allow psychiatric jargon to describe the life of a person with dementia lose meaningful relationship with their person. They tend to dismiss any possibility of admitting there is real meaning to many of the communications and this really takes away possible meaningful exchange between people.

Then, such people often resort to the use of psychiatric medica-tions, which are merely chemical restraints and often very harm-ful to the person with dementia. There are many reports now, coming in from all over the world, demonstrating a high death rate among elders with dementia being wrongly medicated with anti-psychotic drugs.

There are two reasons why people with dementia are given anti-psychotic drugs. One is that their symptoms do not in fact correlate with dementia but are the symptoms of serious mental illness—and this is not rare. I make a guesstimate that about 20 percent of people said to have dementia are actually seriously mentally ill people who have managed to evade the proper clas-sification.

This has often stayed true for them throughout their whole life until old age. They may have been described by family mem bers as having "nerves" or "anger problems" or being "weird" or "difficult," but what they were in reality was seriously mentally

149

ill. This group are mentally ill and act out their illness in bizarre and sometimes threatening behaviors and they do need the help of psychiatric medications.

However, one of the other reasons that elders with dementia get the anti-psychotics which kill them is unskilled caregiver relationships or having a caregiver who is actually mentally ill or in fragile mental stability. Such a caregiver may insist to a doctor that a person needs psychiatric medication and in some care facilities it has long been used as a behavior control easier than training staff to avoid unskillful interventions with residents.

It's a tragedy taking place all over the US, Canada and western Europe right now, so that makes our own integrity as caregivers even more important.

## *Notes to Self*

Frena Gray-Davidson

Speaking Dementia

Frena Gray-Davidson

Speaking Dementia

---

## Dealing With Mom's Doctor

Getting older is a complicated journey. So, it is older patients and their family members who have to undertake the training of their doctors. This doesn't mean I don't like doctors. I do. However, look at the following facts.

1. **Medications** cause 65 percent of all admissions to hospital among elders, not to their illnesses;

2. The average elder is taking anything up to as many as **21 different** medications;

3. **$600,000** is charged in the health costs of an elder in the last six months of life;

4. **Unnecessary procedures** are being visited on those who don't need them and would not want them if they were truly informed. The consequences in suffering are immense.

That's why your Mom needs a good doctor. One who sees her as an individual person. Know that it's okay for you to be asking questions, on behalf of your Mom with dementia.

**How To Train Mom's Doctor** B

**1. Question everything;**

**2. Ask Why.** Know the reason for change in your mother's health routine, especially if she seems to be doing well. Note the answers abd research them afterwards.

**3. Know the Risks of Surgery.** Resist signing her up for routine surgeries that people without dementia do okay with. Especially if they involve general anesthesia;

**4. Seek a second opinion.** A good doctor refers ungrudgingly for a second opinion to guide you and Mom. If the doctor gets miffed, you need a better doctor.

These days, many surgeries are done with an epidural block and other totally numbing medications, exactly because of the dangers of general anesthesia. Even a hip replacement surgery can be done this way.

I have found in my experience that many of those with dementia had also had three general anesthesias over the age of 60. Sometimes, only one can do the damage.

**5. Make wise choices.** Know, as the caregiver of your family member with dementia, that elective medical procedures involving complex rehabilitation may simply not be the best choice for someone with dementia. For example, hip replacement surgery is a huge blessing for the elder who can co-operate, remember and fully take part in the physical rehabilitation.

For the person who doesn't remember that he or she has had the surgery—and that a complex number of warnings and actions apply—it may just become the gateway to almost total physical incapacity.

Of course, if a person falls and breaks a hip, something must be done. However, if it is an elective surgery, maybe it's better NOT to elect it but get a better pain regime.

I'm not giving medical advice here, just filling you in on what dementia means in daily life. You need to question a surgeon closely to know exactly what behaviors and rehab would be required and you need to talk with other caregivers. Then make up your mind.

Doctors want to use their own special expertise. Surgeons want to cut—it's their nature. They don't want you to deal with your back pain through homeopathy, chiropractic, biofeedback, relaxation, exercise, even when it is known to help.

Don't be intimidated. Remember, doctors don't do your dying for you, so you are entitled to your own choices, even if they're unwise.

## 7. Get the general practitioner's help:

Your person's own doctor is often the best person to discuss what specialists tell you. For one thing, they know your mother and from their own experience often understand the caregiver's task better than, say, a surgeon or a kidney specialist.

## 8. Seek Other Solutions:

Ask about other possibilities, such as better pain control or physiotherapy and also research health conditions yourself. These days, it is the patient who needs to learn the most about the whole picture of health conditions.

Get completely informed from as many resources as possible. Look into alternative approaches and see if any of them seem sensible and something your Mom could easily try.

## 9. Know Medication Side Effects:

You must read up on medication side effects and consumer reports on their effects. Use the internet for this, as it will have the most recent responses available. Read up on them, ask your pharmacist about them, get on the Internet and find out what the side effects really are.

## 10. Talk to a pharmacist.

They're always honest, because they aren't defensive about medications since they didn't prescribe them. Make notes on your Mom as she starts a new medication. Notice changes, responses, problems, reactions. Be prepared to ask your doctor for something without unpleasant side effects. Remember, no-one has to take any medication. We all have the right to refuse.

Unless a medication is actually life-saving, don't be afraid to make the final decision yourself on whether your person will take it. Don't accept medication changes when things are going okay. Dr Joe Graedon, Harvard-educated pharmacist, suggests you go for a drug which has been on the market for at least 3 years. By then side-effect reports are in. **Never** accept that handful of free samples your doctor kindly gives you to try.

## 11. Ask for a regular review of your person's medications.

157

Sometimes you may want your Mom to balance out the gains and losses and decide what you both want to do. Yes, your doctor has had a lengthy education in the health of the body, but you are the expert on the person you care for. And you are the gatekeeper keeping harm away.

The best doctor for any elder is the one who respects you have a right to your choices. If you have a sensitive doctor who takes your decisions badly and seems hurt, offended or angry, that isn't the right doctor for an elder.

You see, you even have a right to be wrong.

## *Notes to Self*

---

## Feeding Dementia Food

Henry sneaks ice-cream bars out of the freezer whenever his wife's back is turned. He might have dementia but, by gosh, he knows where the good stuff is kept.

"What can I do to stop him?" his wife asks us at the support group.

Maud, on the other hand, sits and stares at her plate of food, unwilling to eat any of it until her daughter does what's needed.

"She won't eat a damn thing unless I separate all the food into different colors so they don't touch. What the heck is that all about?" she stares round at our support group belligerently.

Ah, the mysteries of dementia ! I think to myself.

When I moved in with Hannah, the first person I ever cared for with Alzheimer's, I noticed she ate all the food on one side of her plate and didn't touch the other side unless I turned the plate round. I also wondered what the heck that was all about. But I was intrigued and I didn't take it personally.

We can simplify the basic issue this way. Our folks have to eat. Studies have shown that people with dementia may use up about 4,000 calories a day. That's a construction guy's calory load. Why they need that much is debatable. My guess is that it is the beleaguered brain, struggling to process thought and memory against the barriers of dementia.

Remember how studying intensely makes you really hungry? Brain work eats up calories. It's well known that people with dementia love their sugar. The brain needs three different kinds of sugars to operate, none from ice-cream, alas.

### Proteins:

We really need elders eating lots of protein and calories. Most of the dietary guidance given by doctors is inadequate if not actually erroneous. So, unless there are real medical reasons to cut out salt, butter, caffeine and sugar from a diet, then just put all that back in. We need to tempt elders to eat. Someone who's already lived to the mid-80s can eat whatever doesn't kill them, so there.

### Step Up Flavor:

We meet the needs of dementia eaters by stepping up flavor, using herbs, spices, molasses, lemons and garlic more. We use real butter, real olive oil, real salt and real eggs to make everything taste better. Have bright colorful foods so things look good on the plate. You can use just tiny amounts of these colors—slender strips of red and orange peppers, thin slices of red apples, sweet oranges.

### Five Meals Daily:

More and smaller meals a day might work better to get someone eating—five little meals rather than three big ones. Give them coffee, if they like it, with caffeine in it. It raises the spirits and it gets the colon working. Not one study shows caffeine is bad for elders

### Respect Dementia Needs:

Respect display needs, even if you don't understand them. Separate the items on the plate, turn the plate round so everything gets eaten. These are probably all brain perception issues.

I've seen over the years small, attractive-looking, colorful plates of food get people eating. Add meat, fruit ,cheese all on the same plate. Always eat together. Maybe take a plate to the sofa, sit together and munch on finger food. It's very soothing and supportive to be there in that way.

Elders may no longer want big slabs of meat but, if they're meat-eaters, they do want meat. So, give them meat. If they'll eat bacon and eggs for breakfast, give it to them. We want them to eat.

The brain cells need fat to work well. So do struggling brain cells, so don't try to put people on fat-deficient diets. It would be great if all our elders with dementia would eat salmon and salad greens, but mainstream elders in America are not those people. And our job is to find food they will eat. Not good food they won't eat. I'm not a fan of Heartland food, but I'm very enthusiastic about people eating.

There are ways to add healthy sugars. You can make fruit bars with real fruit, using unsweetened apple sauce and whole grain flour. Make fruit pies, fruit muffins and use honey, molasses, maple syrup, even prickly pear syrup, as better ways to get sugar. Try fruit smoothies, using organic wholefat yogurt, and add ripe sweet fruit to the plate as a garnish. Sliced peeled apples, orange slices, plums cut into small portions, sliced peaches are all tempting, even added to a meat plate.

As Julia would say, bon appetit!

## Notes to Self

## MAKE YOUR CAREGIVING EASY

Now I'm not saying dementia caregiving is always easy, because it isn't. However, there are a group of consistently
mis-handled issues that every caregiver could easily learn to deal
with better.

How do I know? Because I've facilitated support groups
where these are the issues reported over and over by caregivers.
They are all basic  normal everyday dementia issues— and the
problem? The problem is that caregivers simply cannot or will
not or do not accept them.

It is clear to me that often, the caregiver holds onto to these
struggles because of  their own state of relationship with the
person they're  looking after. A poor relationship, of course,  is
likely to make anger or frustration surface very easily.  Then the
caregiver may feel that  the person with dementia is  deliberately
doing, or not doing, things when they are merely exhibiting the
normal symptoms of their disease.

It can also be the caregiver's relationship with the dementia
that is the issue. Many caregivers feel deep down that it is their
duty to fight the dementia. It's  very hard to accept that there
are things we can't do anything much about. But, right now, on
the whole we can't do very much about dementia. So,  aiming
for a pleasant daily life is  good enough.

Either way, our caregiver stand-off can be  very distressing
and upsetting to the person with dementia. It leaves that person
frightened, upset, lonely and trapped with the feeling they're

not good enough. That dementia is somehow their own fault. It makes them feel like bad people.

So, here are some basic dementia symptoms which we don't have power over—neither the caregiver, nor the person who has the dementia. Rather than fight these, adapt to them. You don't have to accept them, necessarily, but you need to work with them, or you will wear yourself to a frazzle.

**Short-term memory:**

These problems are something over which no-one has control yet caregivers often resist them. Short-term memory loss is the inability to recall things said or done in recent life. The severity may vary, according to the degree of brain deterioration in the memory sector. What caregivers need to accept is that short term memory does not vary because the person chooses it that way. There is no secret message in forgetfulness and their forgetting is not all about you.

163

**Daily variations:**

There can be daily differences connected with brain issues, processing issues, medication issues and general health issues in your person. This is one of those situations where we can apply the guidelines of the 12-Step program. Start with Step One which is that you do not have power over dementia and neither does your person..

If you can't, or won't, accept that, then perhaps you need to ask yourself if you can be a caregiver to this person. Daily happiness is much better goal than useless attempts to fix.

**Mixed memory problems:**

Memory is puzzling to others. People often ask something like "Why doesn't my husband remember I just told him where the dinner plates are, when he can remember every bit of his golf game yesterday?"

Usually said with a mixture of frustration, resentment

and sheer bewilderment. And it's a good question. So I'm going to give you a good answer, based on my understanding of brain memory complexity.

Memory is not stored in just one place in the brain. It's not only stored differently in memory time, with longterm memory safely tucked away in a separate memory vault from short-term memory. It's also stored according to the type of memory it is. If it involves something seen, it might be in visual. If it involved a beautiful tropical garden, maybe the scent of jasmine would be tucked away in the brain under sense information. Parts of the brain where various memories are stored may remain uninjured during the deterioration process typical of dementia.

Plus, and of course here's the really annoying thing for any wife, things liked for a long time that are meaningful and involving, may have more backup to be remembered. Such as yesterday's golf game, which wins over today's dinner plate instructions.

164

That still doesn't mean your husband is deliberately forgetting. Rather it means there are multiple brain areas active to support the memory of the golf game—physical activity brain storage, fun-with-the-guys brain storage which would perhaps be emotional areas, the scores perhaps in the mathematical areas,. So there a lot of storage possibilities which might hold that memory better. Dinner plate orders probably only in short-term memory, which is one place only..

What we can recall and what we can't recall is merely a brain processing issue. So you might as well accept that, rather than make yourself crazy. So, be glad he can still play golf, otherwise you'd get no time to yourself. Next time, you give location orders, point as well. That gives two cues instead of just one, and it may help things go more smoothly.

It's not at all unusual for people with severe dementia to nevertheless have great longterm recall. They can talk about being in the one-room schoolhouse so long ago, who was there, their names, what they did, every tiny detail. And if you checked on it, you'd find it was accurate recall.

How can they do that when they've apparently forgotten the last fifteen years, including this morning? It's that brain storage thing again. Longterm memories are stored in a different party of the brain, plus they're longterm. They're deeply embedded.

People with dementia also get that memory intensification that most elders get, in which their past is often more present than your present. Partly that's the embedded nature of those memories, but also I see it as **where the work of memory needs to be done.** It's the nature of old humans to be considering the years, times and people that made them. There is a deep and intuitive human journey of memory which goes on and still goes on also for those with dementia.

It's a reconciliation quest so powerful and so deep that few can resist its insistence as life draws to a close, whether they have dementia or not.

People without dementia take up writing their life story and studying their genealogy, while people with dementia go to live with Mom and Dad long ago. They reside in that time zone for long periods of time. And, however bad their present day memory, they may have extraordinary and accurate memories of back then, complete with names, stories and occasions. To me, watching them at memory work, it's a sacred journey towards peace.

Dementia wounds the parts of the brain that control rational thinking. This means people with dementia simply cannot do the step-by-step process of rational thinking, because brain flow is blocked.

No point in trying to win a logical argument with them. You get angry, your person fearful. The best management tool is to stop trying to make this person agree you are right and they are wrong. Stop trying to win. You are already the the winner.

You don't have dementia. You won, okay? Don't deliberately follow a path that only leads to more frustration. Instead, ask yourself why you are trying to force a bewildered old person to admit they're wrong and you're right. What's really bothering you?

What about your difficult feelings -- fear, disgust and guilt-ridden inner drive to take on a task you don't want to do? Let me tell you something. Your family member would have a much nicer time in life without you IF you don't take responsibility for yourself and seek your own healing.

So, if you can't connect with your own inner lovely person and be kind, relaxed, accepting or forgiving—at least on some kind of regular basis—then please stop tormenting your family member and let them live in peace in a really nice little care home, okay?

One thing I will promise you, if you decide to take on your own inner struggle with honesty and a wish to resolve it, the rewards are huge. Good caregivers are very different from everyone else. That's all I'm going to say about that.

**166**

## *Notes to Self*

---

## DEMENTIA SOCIAL LIFE

Your Grandma has changed since she was diagnosed with Alzheimer's. It's not just the memory thing. You could under stand that. She just doesn't seem to be as social as she used to be. You wonder if she's depressed. Maybe you should make her continue her old routine. Or should you?

As a longterm dementia caregiver, I see lots of wishful thinking going on in families. Typically, the family wants a good life to continue for their elder with dementia. Of course. They think it would help to bring back former joys. And secretly they hope it will restore health.

In reality, though, people with dementia don't change their social life because they forgot what they used to like. No, your Grandma has changed her social pattern because she no longer feels comfortable in it. It's hard for people with dementia to keep up with all that's required in a group.

You can do it, now. But someone struggling with following even one conversation finds it too stressful. So, Grandma is just developing a style that allows slower, less stressful interaction. She may be happier with one or two people now. She may do well with a pet, even if she never had one before. She might prefer one-to-one social activities. She may do better with becoming more an onlooker than a participant.

You all feel sorry for her. You see her life as reduced and more empty. You want to refill it. However, a recent study carried out in England demonstrated that, because people with dementia forget they aren't following their one-time routine, they still feel as if they're doing the same stuff.

They feel the same sense of connection, links to pleasure and emotional richness as if they were still doing the stuff they enjoyed. Now, THAT's odd and intriguing, isn't it?

What Grandma needs is for the family to help her figure what works for her NOW. Something that works with the fact that she has cognitive and memory impairment. That means taking her places, doing things and noting what really does work for her. Doing your research, with Grandma. Ask one of her old friends if they'll be part of the new care plan too.

It often takes changing your expectations of Grandma, without judgment. Your adjustment will be worth it. Get family members to put their own unrealistic wishes, hopes and opinions aside. Look for clues from the past and adapt them to her present. One woman I knew was famed as a wonderful quilter. With increasing dementia, she clearly did not want to do that because she couldn't.

**168**

I introduced her to coloring books, using the wonderful adult coloring books that the Dover Books publish. It seemed to me that, since she had dealt in color, patterns and designs, it might fill the gap. And it did. She became a coloring fan and happily spent hours daily for the next three years of her life doing just that. It was something to do which touched on her interests and created a thoughtful, meditative routine for her which seemed to bring her a lot of inner satisfaction.

As family members, we have to be willing to give up our well-meant but selfish wishes that Grandma be as good as ever. Then, we can really help her have the life she's now capable of. It takes experimenting and some patience, but it's really worth it. And there'll still be plenty of enjoyment ahead. Don't forget to involve the younger family members. They may be more open-minded and inventive about the plan to keep Grandma occupied. What you're really doing is making a care plan. And because you do care, together you'll find the one that works.

## The Poop Factor in Dementia

A care manager friend of mine describes it as the biggest issue in whether a family opt for a long-term care placement or keeping Mom at home with the family. She calls it the Poop Factor. It is one of the most emotionally-fraught issues in personal care of family elders. In our society, there is a special disgust around grownups needing such help.

The myth of incontinence in dementia is that everyone with dementia has incontinence. Actually, that's not at all true. True incontinence, as in real loss of body control, affects only about 10 percent of people with dementia. The other 90 percent usually suffer from one of three problems.

They forget how to recognize the body signal to go the bathroom and are unable to find the bathroom anyway. They may also have digestion issues which could be eased and medication side effects. Sudden incontinence is often due to a Urinary Tract Infection (UTI), especially in women.

Assuming you have taken your person to the doctor for a check-up and there are no physical reasons to account for incontinence, then you need your plan. It's pretty simple. You have a regular reminder schedule to get your person to the bathroom. When you want your person to go to the bathroom, be sure not to ask if he or she would like to go, because that allows for the answer, "No."

Instead, suggest it. As in, "Let's get you to the bathroom now," followed with a swift bribe, "Then you'll be ready for lunch (a nap, a movie, whatever)."

This regular reminder may be all that is needed. Maybe once

every two hours or possibly more frequently, will cover it. And don't order anyone about, by the way. Everyone hates that— you, people without dementia and people with dementia. No-one likes bossiness. And you don't want to be upsetting someone who's going to the bathroom, okay? And you don't want to evoke resistance either, which bossiness does.

The effective language of dementia is suggestion, persuasion and inclusiveness. It's a "let's all go" attitude, not a "you must do" command.

The rest of the approach is to have all the right equipment in the bathroom. Everything from a raised toilet seat, to generous supplies of protective underwear and please stop calling them "diapers" for goodness' sake. You also need protective gloves for you, generous amounts of wipes, for Grandma, plenty of soft toilet paper, a big garbage can with a big garbage bag in it.

I can do this now, so you certainly can. When I began looking after elders, dealing with the poop factor made me literally whimper with panic and silently pray.

But I'm okay now. Not enthused, ever. But I can do it and so can you. Always consider whether diarrhea is due to medication issues, since many medications have diarrhea as a side effect. Additionally, many elders are just taking too many medications, a number of them all doing the same thing so that the body is trying, wisely, to eradicate this toxin from the system. Read up on medications, note side effects and any duplication of un-wanted effects. You know, if one stool softener is good, two are not better.

See the doctor with a list of questions to ask. Point out the difficulty of incontinence and negotiate the doctor down on the medications if you can. I know you're not a doctor, okay? But you are the poop-attendant-in-chief and diarrhea is a real medical issue with serious side effects. It's okay to ask about eliminating its causes. A good doctor will redesign the medication approach to deal with the problems, if possible.

If the doctor gets miffed, huffy or stuffy about this—you and Grandma need a better doctor. Good doctoring is never about ego, it's about the best care for an elder. Much of that is able to be negotiated.

Sometimes digestion problems are the issue. Most people have to change their eating habits as they age. Food and drink affect people differently. They often can no longer eat the same things as they did when younger. Hard-to-digest food will cause problems. Meat is often less digestible as elders chew less well and lose their natural digestive enzymes.

In my care home, we had an old gentleman who always had diarrhea for four days after his family took him out for a steak dinner. His system could no longer deal with.

This can be a good place to bring on the digestive enzymes and use them after checking it's okay with your person's doctor. Then follow up with chicken and ham, instead of steak. Don't be embarrassed to keep going back for the solution. Continuous diarrhea is bad in every way for an elder.

Urinary tract infections are common in elders and can often have no other symptom than sudden urinary incontinence. Although a UTI in a younger person is often a side-effect of sexual activity, in an elder it often results from never sufficiently emptying the bladder. The continual residue makes a happy germ pool within, also a sign of a poor immune system.

In older women, it is most often due to the practice of wiping toilet paper from back to front and thus drawing fecal bacteria into the vagina. Women with dementia seem especially prone to this practice, which is why supervision in the bathroom is a very good idea.

In my own work and in my care homes, we found that with a care plan in place, a schedule and some monitoring, we could keep people UTI-free almost all the time.

## How To Argue With Dementia

Here is how to win the argument in dementia. Ready? Okay. This is what you say, to win.

"Uh-huh."

"Oh, I see."

"Really?"

"I didn't know that."

"Well, my goodness."

And so on. I'm sure you get the idea. The idea is, in case you didn't get it, not to argue. Because you won't win. Neither will your person. That person can't follow logic and rational presentation of ideas to prove something, usually that they're wrong. But they do know when you're trying to make them wrong and that upsets them.

Now, I know you're not trying to make your Mom wrong, right? Or are you? In which case, you won't win. It's the classic dementia no-win, no-win situation. A standoff that upsets everyone.

Try instead, Frena's classic no-say, no-say approach. Your Mom tells you her Dad came to see her last night. Instead of getting all freaked out and arguing—because, actually, dead people do come to see those they love and it's a very normal experience— you take a different approach.

"Oh really?" you say. Now would it kill you to say that? I'd hope you'd say it to a little child who told you she met a talking frog in the garden. So you can say it to your Mom with dementia.

"Oh really?" is a neutral comment. It neither implies endorsement nor condemnation. It's just a receptive grunt signaling, " I heard that."

Most of the things people argue about in dementia don't need an argument. Worse, it promotes real arguments, with frustration and upset for both parties. If you need your person to go somewhere or do something, use the grown-up dementia management technique and don't even discuss it. Don't even ask. Don't even tell.

Let me show you how that works.

**Doctor Appointment:** Mom has a doctor's appointment, which you made. Allow plenty of time, offer her a nice ride in the car and help her get dressed. Into the car. Drive. Arrive at the doctor's office. In you both go and there you are.

**Shower:** If you need Mom to have a shower, offer the help without asking her if she'd like a shower. Instead, you say, "I'm getting the shower ready now so we can go out for a drive."

The basic deal here is to offer a suggestion and inducement for it to work. More people these days are telling me they get right in that shower with Mom and that this helps a lot. It might feel weird to you at first, but it isn't really and you can wear your swim gear if you want to.

The purpose of all is for you to get what you want, usually through low cunning and deviousness—and nothing wrong with that. It's called dementia management.

## Notes to Self

173

*Sundowning*

## THE SUNDOWNING PLAN

No-one truly knows what causes sundowning. There are a number of theories, but really those theories don't help us very much. Luckily, that does not stop you coming up with a great sundowning care plan that works.

That's because the one fact you do know is the person you care for. Assuming that what you're dealing with really is dementia, and not mental illness or PTSD for example, then this care plan will help. For some families, it has entirely resolved the issue. In others, it has made it more manageable. Here is the Sundowning Care Plan which I have evolved and which has positive results, ranging from good to excellent.

A good care plan is based on a number of factors.

1. **Accurate observation** of the person we know;

2. **Knowledge of physical and emotional care** needed for that person;

3. **Caregivers skills.**

4. **A distraction plan.**

You need to become an unbiased observer for a few days. Make notes. Set aside your confusion and any assumptions you've made. Just watch—whilst also being the caregiver, of course. Someone else's sundowning is absolutely not about you.

Study your person's sundowning. Note time, sequence, emotional themes, behaviors and winding down. Make notes for several days, until you know the pattern. Don't jump to conclusions and don't put your ego there.

Don't write "She does this to drive me crazy!" but "Very agitated between 5pm and 7pm." Do your usual appropriate caregiving, while being the calm observer. You may learn something new when you keep calm, even though your person is not.

Listen carefully to what this person says and make notes on that. You may find out painful truths about how it feels to be that person with dementia. Listen with your heart, don't argue and instead just be kind, soothing and respectful.

"I'm sorry you feel so alone — that must be scary."

When they want to go home, don't argue but say something like, "I know, you miss home, don't you?"

**Calming Sundowning:**

**1. More Sleep:**

People with dementia have increased brain activity all the time, even in sleep. Brain studies confirm this. So they need lots of help in the form of sleep, food and drink. Lack of these may contribute to extra emotional meltdown.

**176**

Work on increasing your person's sleep time—ideally 8 hours overnight, plus after-lunch nap. Little cat-naps during the day are okay too. Don't believe people who say you have to keep your person awake all day so they can sleep at night.

It is very exhausting having dementia. That exhaustion is often the cause of being unable to sleep at night. They are too tired to be able to relax and fall asleep.

**2. More Food:**

One hour before sundowning usually starts, give a nutritious snack and both water and possibly a fruit drink.

**3. Lavender oil:**

Use pure lavender essential oil to help emotional calmness. Add ten drops to about half a pint of water, and spray the room, the sofa, you —but probably not the person.

**4. Calm yourself :**

Breathe deep and slow, relax muscles, choose to be calm.

You may be asked difficult questions, like "Where is my mother?"

The real-time answer is "dead'. This is not useful, however, so just be evasive, persuasive, using redirection and a good distraction. Meanwhile, understand that asking about mother is dementia code for someone feeling frightened, lost, lonely and abandoned.

Don't try to fix these, because you can't. Those are real feelings, based in the here-and-now reality of how it sometimes feels to have dementia. Just respond supportively"I'm here. I'll help you."

Or don't say anything—just put an arm round your person, hold hands or just lean against them soothingly.

Agitation is catching, so don't catch it. Breathe calmly. Remind yourself that this will pass.

If you get really caught up, there is something in you that needs your attention. Caregivers most distressed by sundowning often have unresolved relationships with their person. If so, it's time to start resolving. Few sundowning people really need psychiatric and behavior control drugs. Those are most commonly enforced by caregivers who are themselves in psychological distress.

Don't let this be you. Get into therapy, read self-help books, practice forgiveness. Have a good book to read. Everyone has their solution. Find yours. Understand that your person is in fact doing the special work of finding peace and resolution by expressing longtime sadness, losses, and angers.

We hear all the time that people with dementia are empty or like the living dead, which of course they aren't. People who say these things are either overwhelmed emotionally by the task of caregiving or they are just dementia bigots. Ignore them. Use the tools of unconditional love, adding forgiving of your person and yourself.

People withd ementia are doing the same great life review that most other elders are. Some of the distress they suffer is that no-one near them wants to hear all this.

Remember, crying never hurt anyone. It's hurt that drives crying. Not the other way round. Weeping helps us adapt to and let go of sorrow. So don't be frightened by an old person's tears. Instead, feel privileged to be their witness.

Many elders with dementia have unfinished emotional issues. Crying, grief or anger. So you can let them do this, and then move to your entertainment plan. A drive, a favorite DVD, dancing the tango, dinner on the table—whatever works.

## *Notes to Self*

## THE MYSTERY OF SUNDOWNING

Sundowning can be a regular part of any dementia. It's that time, usually towards later afternoon and early evening, when the person with dementia may become emotionally upset, angry, tearful and cannot be consoled.

Sometimes caregivers report that they fear actual violence from their person. Others claim that sundowning actually goes on all night, even accompanied by physical destruction of the environment.

What the heck is going on here, do I hear you ask? Why, yes, I think I do. So let me stick my non-medical opinion in here—based on 20 years of Alzheimer's caregiving and fifteen years of hearing other caregivers talking about their lives on the battle-front.

First, no-one actually knows what causes sundowning. Doctors guess at the reduction of daylight, with brain chemicals responding to that, lack of calming serotin in the brain and other medically-brainy stuff. So here's my take—and before you go pooh-pooh, let me tell you that putting my sundowning plan into affect has reduced sundowning in people with dementia from 50 percent to gone.

You know, some version of sundowning occurs in most human beings when tired, stressed, hungry, alone. Babies are often fractious at this time. Depressed people become more so at this time. Birds go out on the big fly-around before nightfall.

The coming of night is a very big thing in nature. It somewhat affects every human being, since we too are in fact part of nature. No surprise then that it effects people with dementia.

Your person used to have a life. A woman was typically preparing the evening meal for her family, a man was returning from work after a hard day, the kids came back from school. A lot happened in the sunset hours.

Now it doesn't. Yet this person's life had a particular rhythm to it for many decades. That may be over, but the pattern of feeling and habit is not over. Old women with dementia still feel that their children are coming home for that vital shared meal of dinner—even though those children are in their seventies.

The loss of working short-term memory leaves old people stranded on the river of time without an anchor.

The perfectly reasonable logical thing that happens when a person is no longer anchored to today by memory is to go to where **memory is longest and strongest.** That is mainly the past and especially the past of living at home with Mom and Dad. It's not craziness. It's what happens when normal short-term memory is disrupted. Never argue with them. Just listen and pay attention to what you hear.

Don't be dismissive and insensitive to what once made life worthwhile and now no longer exists. It's a loss, a sense of emptiness and loneliness which is very distressing to the person we care for. It's very hard work to have dementia, to be struggling to remember, to make sense of things. To lose relevance and meaning. All brain studies show the dementia brain is over-active, not less active. So in the sun-downing plan, we are trying to reduce the stress and pain of our person.

180

The stress-reduction plan should include more rest, longer hours of sleep in the morning, perhaps an after-lunch nap. More to do while awake. A snack and a drink an hour before sundowning time. You calm and not agitated. We caregivers, being caring people, often get far too upset in sundowning time. We catch agitation. We feel the desperation. We get overwhelmed, just like our person.

We need inner calm, knowing the this sundowning tantrum-weeping time is like toddler's supermarket fit. No harm is done. Sundowning and being upset doesn't harm. It just upsets.

## Notes to Self

## WHAT TO DO ABOUT SUNDOWNING

What are we supposed to do about sundowning? You know, that time of emotional upheaval, wild distress and sometimes great anger that occurs usually in late afternoon. What can we caregivers do to help? It's a good question and much better than "How can we stop Mom from sundowning?"

Caregivers get very caught up in the struggle to do the impossible— to stop sundowning, though I have to qualify that statement. In fact, it is possible to stop sundowning, but it's not done in one afternoon. Effective planning reduces, modifies and ultimately may indeed prevent sundowning, but that needs time, thought and a structured approach.

Most caregivers, when they ask how they can stop sundowning in their family members, really mean "How can we switch this behavior right off?"

So, the very first thing we need to do is to understand what sundowning is. Then why it is. Fnally how it is and what to do about that.

Make sure you know if Grandpa has dementia or whether he is actually dealing with a serious mental illness, like schizophrenia, bipolar disorder, psychosis or maybe just an untreated urinary tract infection. Or even a recent change of medication. Or does he have PTSD from his wartime experiences in the Philippines or a brutal childhood? Many of these apply to many families.

Sundowning is a limited period of agitation and emotional distress experienced on a regular basis by a person diagnosed as having dementia. It usually occurs towards the end of the day, from late afternoon and possibly extending to darkness. Hence the term "sundowning".

Why does it happen? Medical answers are largely guesswork. Some researchers suggest it is due to decreasing light at the end of the day which causes confusion and emotional misinterpretation in those with dementia.

The medical researchers who approach it from the loss-of-light-intensity angle suggest you use full spectrum lighting in your house, especially at the hours when your person has been known to have sundowning. And some improvement has been reported through this, plus the use of melatonin pills given earlier in the day. Those are always worth a try.

As a caregiver, I've managed to make effective intervention plans for people with dementia who have regularly experienced the sundowning syndrome. As always in dementia, there isn't just one answer to this. There is a mix of answers, and then there is your person, who is also an individual. Sundowning care plans are not a one-fits-all deal, but neither is dementia.

Everyone does dementia in his or her own way, and the same is true of sun-downing. That's why we need a multi-faceted approach.

Fatigue is definitely an issue since it is very exhausting to be an elder with dementia. See where you can help reduce that with more sleep, more relaxation and better nutrition. Enough fluids in the system play a major part in reducing dementia and helping someone stay calm. Lots of water throughout the day, in small glassfuls, with constant cuing.

Give a nutritious snack, with a fruit drink, about an hour before sundowning usually starts to keep up the calory count. Also think about whether about 5 little meals would work better than the traditional three big ones. That might well be better for you too. If you don't know or aren't sure how to change your dietary approach google it or get dietary books from your

183

library.

At workshops, caregivers often ask if sundowning is craziness and of course the answer is no. But mental illness is not unheard of among elders said to have dementia. At a conservative guess, I would estimate that up to 20 percent of elders said to have dementia actually do have serious mental illnesses, like paranoid schizophrenia or a bipolar condition.

One of the problems is that while some dementias have their own name and detectable physical markers, many others do not. If you know from family history that your person has had a mental illness condition, or is suspected to have one, then violent acting out or frightening hallucinations may be a manifestation of that illness. Especially prolonged night-time behaviors.

A lot of elders who have dementia experience sundowning, but by no means all. For a bystander, sundowning can be upsetting. After all, if it's your Mom, you might find it hard to take her weeping anxiety attacks calmly. She's your Mom. You want to help. Most of all, you want to stop those two sorrow-laden hours before dinner being a sob-fest of shoulder-shaking proportions. You want her to stop wailing for her Mom to come home.

Or maybe it's your Dad who does the sundowning thing. You find him crouching inside a closet, hiding out from unknown enemies with guns.

"Don't tell them I'm here!" he says hoarsely, as you softly bang your head against the wall, asking yourself if he's crazy.

Well, is he? Your Mom or your Dad or your spouse or mean old Auntie Nell. Are any of them crazy? It's our job to help get the right diagnosis for our folks. If things seem extreme, get that person to a psychiatrist and let the doctor decide. Then you can really get the help your person needs. Now that is good care-giving.

## How To Know It's Sundowning

It's a regular period of emotional upset and neediness daily;
It occurs at pretty much the same time each day;

It often has the same themes—loss, loneliness, uselessness, fear, longing for dead family members;

It often refers to life traumas suffered by this person—childhood abuse, a death, wartime experience;

It stops after a regular period of time, typically about two hours. So the person with sundowning moves back to normal dementia life, but caregivers often remain caught up in the emotional drama. Worn out and fearful of the next time.

The most important thing that almost everyone totally ignores. about sundowning is that it IS a period of time when people are really looking at old stuck pain and fear and loss and trauma. People are working things through that weigh on their hearts. They may cry, or be angry. Then they have dinner.

How can you tell if their sundowning is normal or if its craziness?

**How To Tell Sundowning from Crazy:**

1. **Sundowning has time limits**, but crazy goes on all night long;

2.**Sundowning is emotional**, but things don't get broken;

3. **Sundowning does not physically attack you**, where crazy might;

4.**Sundowning has a timetable**, but crazy doesn't;

5.**Sundowning can be frightened** but crazy is paranoid.

Sundowning needs your patience, kindness and smarts. Crazy needs good psychiatrists and possibly psych meds. Hope that helps.

## *Notes to Self*

_____

## MANAGING SUNDOWNING

After memory problems, probably sundowning is one of the issues to most upset caregivers of people with dementia. That's because they see it as upsetting the person they care for. And they feel helpless.

Unfortunately, many caregivers too are driven to tears by other people's sundowning. So, I'd like you to dry your tears, at least for the moment, while I share some interesting sundowning know-how with you.

Firstly, no-one really knows why people sundown. We can surmise. It comes towards the end of daylight, typically, though people vary. Most people who do sundown do it in the afternoon into sunset, hence the term sundowning. A typical time pattern would be 4pm to 6pm, 5 to 7pm, and so on.

Sundowning usually lasts for a couple of hours and people tend to have the same approximate pattern. So Uncle George might sundown in late afternoon on a regular basis, while the lady down the road gets upset after dark for a period of time. Meanwhile, Mrs Gonzalez has a time of being upset and tearful in the morning. So, there are patterns but no absolute rules.

Except for this one. **Rampaging around all night long is NOT sundowning.** Normal dementia sundowning is of limited duration. Extended hours of after-dark chaos and destruction needs the expert input of a psychiatrist to find out exactly what is going on.

The kinds of background that typically involve lengthy episodes or terror, rage or destruction may be due to undiagnosed serious mental illness, maybe **schizophrenia** or **bipolar disorders.**

It may be caused by serious **allergic reactions** to opiates or other medications being given, ironically enough, to calm and help an often anxious person.

It may also be due to **PTSD**, in retired military or survivors of childhood sexual abuse or other major traumas.

I'm not trying to diagnose here, just urging families dealing with extended violent acting-out episodes to seek expert medical help. Don't believe people who tell you this is sundowning, because it is NOT normal sundowning.

Most people I've personally known and heard from by email report to me that they do get the skilled help they need from psychiatrists. So, don't be afraid to ask.

In any dementia situation at all where care needs exceed a normal person's ability to manage the care, it really is a sign that there is something extra going on. You need expert help. Fortunately, most people who have dementia also have Medicare, so that help and the experts are available to you at modest or no cost at all. Never hesitate to seek expert guidance.

So what about a Sundowning Plan?

While we don't know definitively what causes sundowning, there are patterns to guide us:

Babies and toddlers are often fractious too at the day's end; It's also very exhausting to have dementia, which we caregivers forget.;

Children behave worst when tired and hungry. So we may assume that tiredness and hunger are factors;

Lack of hydration makes a recognizable difference too. So, we can reasonably assume that weariness, hunger and thirst are present in the person who is sundowning.

People with dementia are constantly dealing with the past, which they experience as being the present. The feelings during sundowning are real—fear, sadness, loss, anxiety.

After all, wouldn't YOU experience all of those if you had dementia? Here's my Five-Point Plan for you to focus on.

Track the pattern for at least a week so you know the timetable. Give food and drink one hour before the usual beginnings of sundowning.

Be ready to sit calmly while your person weeps, or is anxious or gets angry and accusing. Remind yourself: This too shall pass. Try activities—photo albums of old-time family members, favorite music, drive in the car.

Be affectionate. Don't fix their feelings—you can't. Empathize, support, witness their truth.

## Notes to Self

## MAKING SENSE OF SUNDOWNING

As you might expect from the term "sundowning", this is something which happens typically towards the end of the day and possibly during hours of darkness.

It's not a disease in itself. It's a passing agitation which happens to people who have dementia, whether Alzheimer's dementia or one of the many other dementias of old age.

Sundowning is a regular period of intense emotional upset, usually occurring at roughly the same time each day and lasting typically for a couple of hours. During this time, although the person with dementia doesn't understand why he or she feels this way, the person feels upset, lonely, angry and may dwell on particular events or people of the past. In fact,people may be convinced they ARE living in that past time, not because they're crazy, but because they simply don't remember what day, date and year this is. And you, Missy, won't be able to argue them out of that past time, so don't even try. Let it go. Remember, the feelings are real.

There is deep emotional work to do in that long-ago time. Every older person does this. Long-term memory involvement often intensifies with age and can even remain accurate, despite dementia. So, things from long-ago can be recalled, often with astonishing accuracy, since long-term memory is situated elsewhere in the human brain, not in the frontal lobe where short-memory resides and is injured.

The only major complication of this is that the person with intense long-term memories may be unable to realize they are long-ago. It is the intensity which draws them in and their fractured short-term memory which strands them there. It's not crazy, it's how memory works.

You will not be able to argue them out of their conviction or their longings while the intensification has them held back in time. No need to, either. Just listen, comfort and be kind.

I f they say, at this time, they want to go home, don't argue with them and tell them where they are now IS home. Obviously, it doesn't feel that way or they wouldn't want to go home.

Just comfort them by acknowledging their feelings, as in "Of course you do," and "I know —you miss your Mom, don't you?" Let them talk, weep, tell you long boring memory tales—it's all good. Even the tears are good. They'll settle much more calmly after tears.

I know many caregivers find it as upsetting as the person with dementia does. In fact, it is emotionally difficult to find a calm center within while someone we care for is tearful, angry, emotional or afraid. Agitation is a particularly contagious emotion.

191

This is probably why so many caregivers regard sundowning as the most difficult part of their caregiving load. One reason why this is so is undoubtedly because caregivers CARE. So they are bound to care even more about their person being upset, weepy or angry. Caregivers want to fix what's wrong. That the nature of caregiving.

The most useful approach to dealing with sundowning is to make a care plan for yourself. When we can hold our own center in calmness, then we aren't as easily thrown by other people's emotional states. So the first stage in dealing with sundowning is our own self-care approach to being prepared.

For that, we need to make notes several days in succession as sundowning occurs. These will include noting the usual time and duration of the sundowning, the usual behaviors of agitation, weeping or anger. Also notice the issues raised by the person who is sundowning, such as feeling useless, lonely or abandoned by parents. Experiment to see what helps—food or drink, affection, a walk, a drive—and add that to the notes.

Finally, notice how it winds down and what emotional state the person is in at the end. Many people become quite calm finally. This reminds you that maybe, just maybe, you could sit it out without getting all upset yourself.

**Five-Point Plan for Self-Care:**

1 **Review you notes** so you know what to expect;

2 **Sit calmly;**

3 **Breathe** slow easy breaths and resolve to take nothing personally;

4 **Repeat as necessary.** When your person's sundowning reactions throw you off your calm, start with (1) and (2) again;

5 **Remind** yourself, sundowning passes.

Know that sundowning doesn't hurt people. They may cry or be emotionally upset, but that is closer to a child's tantrum than to an adult's emotional breakdown. The mature parent doesn't get upset by a toddler's meltdown in the supermarket. That's not because they don't care. It's because they understand this is just a passing childlike thing, not a permanent state of being.

In a certain way, the sundowning emotional meltdown comes nearer to childlike overwhelm of feeling than to deep and persistent adult suffering. And we know this because sundowning passes and the person is pretty much okay until the next day's sundowning.

Be very hesitant about drugging your person. Typically, doctors may prescribe anti-psychotics for a dementia meltdown. These, alas, are a guaranteed way to shorten the life of your person, as studies from all over the world are now demonstrating. Anti-psychotics are not appropriate medications for elders with dementia.

I know people say it calms them down, but so would a 2x4 round the side of the head. And that's not legal.

Frena Gray-Davidson

Learning to sit with it, without being swept away yourself, is the beginning of sundowning wisdom. Keep breathing calmly.

## Notes to Self

## Can We Fix Dementia Sundowning?

There's nothing like sundowning to make caregivers feel crazy. And, they aren't any better in care facilities either, believe me. Care staff deal just as badly or just as well with sundowning as you do at home.

However, you can make a plan that works to reduce and even stop sundowning, or at least avoid it being such a nuisance. Try it, because a good plan really works. It takes trial and error and being flexible. Remember, you aren't trying to control agitation. You're trying to bring genuine ease and comfort to someone's distress —a very different goal.

First, we have to be sure we are really dealing with sundowning. Normal sundowning is a period of emotional agitation, typically lasting for a couple of hours and usually beginning towards the end of the afternoon. Although, some families report their person having morning sundowning. During that time, the person may be tearful, frightened, sometimes angry, demanding, or just unhappy and a bit weepy.

If the caregiver stays calm, this helps dementia emotions. Unfortunately, in some families, the caregiver gets as upset as the person with dementia and the outcome can be the use of powerful behavior-controlling drugs. These are often very harmful to the health of an elder with dementia. Using behavioral control drugs is seldom necessary in an elder with dementia who has sundowning. Sadly, their use under such circumstances often reflects the caregiver's problems.

On the other hand, we find elders with serious mental illnesses being tossed into dementia classifications just because it's convenient. How do we know if we're dealing with someone who needs psychiatric workup?

Such elders have extended hours of so-called sundowning. They may be wildly active all night long, violently breaking things, piling furniture up to barricade themselves in their rooms, attacking their roommate or their caregivers.

These abnormal behaviors urgently need expert investigation, because these elders can be dangerous, to themselves, to their caregivers and family members and to other residents in care facility settings. Normal sundowning responds well to a multifaceted approach easy to put into place and rewards consistency by working well.

First, the caregiver notes the time and format of the sundowning. For example, suppose Mildred gets restless and agitated each afternoon at about 3pm, becoming calm again at about 5pm. Her sundowning includes weeping insistence on seeing her mother. She berates her caregiver, sometimes she paces.

How can a caregiver help someone like Mildred?

**Four Ways to Help Sundowning**

**1. Hydration:** Ensure that Mildred has an after-lunch snack and drinks juice and water about an hour before sundowning begins;

**2. Calmness:** Change the environment itself by diffusing pure essential oil of lavender throughout the afternoon. This is notably successful in care units, failing only because staff do not consistently use it.

**3. Music:** It is also effective to have either age-appropriate music or something very soothing playing;

**4. Distraction:** Family photos, going for a drive, watching a favorite dvd, making cookies, taking a walk, playing with pets. Experiment and don't be afraid to fail while looking for what will succeed. If Mildred can't be calmed, then walking with her

195

while she vents her feelings is also fine.

As much as it may bother you to have a weeping angry old person blaming you for what isn't your fault, it actually does not hurt them. In fact, an hour or so of cathartic release can be of great emotional benefit to that elder. Remember, these are largely people who have never been to therapy, ever.

Sundowning often brings release and the unloading of stuff long-held and long-concealed. You become the witness of those secrets. Even if you feel overwhelmed, practice pretending to be calm, kind and wise. That way, you'll actually become all those things.

Consider also, is Mildred getting the rest she needs? People with dementia are often exhausted and this may also be why some of them don't sleep well. It's like over-tired children too hyper to sleep. If this is your Mildred, she might need to go to bed earlier, get up later or have an after-lunch nap or all three.

**196**

This complex care plan can produce very good results. Some people stop sundowning altogether. Others become calmer and easier to manage. It works in care facilities—if staff are encouraged to be consistent—and at home.

Nothing could be more worthwhile than building a plan to ease the emotional struggles of an elder with dementia and it's not hard to do. It just asks you to stay centered while they whirl around. That will grow your own inner being too.

That's the pay-off for you.

## *Notes to Self*

———————————

## How to Handle Sundowning Problems

One of the most challenging issues for Alzheimer's dementia caregivers is meeting head-on the behaviors of sundowning.

Well, that's usually because people ARE trying to meet them head-on. There's a less confrontational way to approach the whole issue. In general, that head-on thing is notably unsuccessful in dealing with dementia. People with dementia are already pretty frightened, insecure people—why else do you think everyone else you know is terrified of having dementia?

Then, there are brain processes which are simply not on-track in dementia.

### Three Can'ts of Dementia

1. **Can't argue** successfully, because their rational thinking process has been disabled by their disease;

2. **Can't remember** what you just told them, so it's just no good telling them again. And again. And again.

3. **Can't recall** the recent past in any reliable way.

All this means that you can't deal with their sundowning by lecturing, hectoring or nagging. A really un-useful thing to say would be, "Now remember yesterday at this time....?"

Instead, since YOU remember yesterday at sundowning time, YOU make the plans. Here's what we think goes on in sundowning. People are both tired and hungry by that time of the day. They feel insecure and anxious. They have feelings which they can't understand. They have needs which they can't express. Then they act all this out.

Their mix of fear, sadness, confusion and overwhelm may really get YOU going, as well as them.

So your job is: **chill out, breathe deep** and don't give way to their upsetness and apply the **Great Sundowning Plan**. Who invented it? Me. Why? Because in 20 years of caregiving, I've seen lots of kinds of sundowning and I've lived to write this for you. So here we go.

**The Great Sundowning Plan:**

**1. Timing:** Know when sundowning usually begins and ends;

**2. Feed and hydrate:** Give a nutritious snack, a fruit drink and also water about an hour and a half before sundowning

**3. Activities:** Prepare your activity plan, which might be going out for a drive (oh yes, and don't forget to take them with you!), watching a special program or movie, looking at family albums of long-ago people—whatever.

**4. Emotional themes:** Be ready for your person's theme and respond appropriately.

Most sundowning people have a very personal emotional theme, around their sense of loss and confusion. Maybe they're waiting for their Mom to come home for dinner. Maybe they tell you how useless they are, maybe they get worked up about a loss or cause of emotional pain.

Because you've studied them closely—right?—and figured all this out, you're ready, with the answers that say you are really listening to them. Helpful responses to sundowning themes:

"I'm sorry you miss your Dad so much right now.";

"Your Mom? I haven't seen her here today.";

"It's okay, I'm here."

You're supporting emotionally. With kindness. You're evading issues— that Mom's Mom is dead, for example. You're just supporting her in her painful need for her Mom. Don't try to "fix" anything. How could you? Can you produce her Mom? Can you make that stillborn baby not have happened? That Dad not have been abusive?

Of course not. Things did happen. The past has gone long ago. So, what could you fix about all that?

I'm glad you asked, because I do know the answer to that. You can fix the loneliness by being there with them and responding in a way that assures them you understand. Words like, "I'm so sorry," "That must have been so scary," even words like, "Wow," "Oh," and "Really?" said with respectful attention can do a great deal to help a lonely soul.

If you don't think so, that's because you haven't stood beside enough hurting people yet. The more you have, the less you might say but the more those well-chosen brief words will reach out to someone. This kind of sundowning usually lasts for approximately anything from one to three hours, then tends to subside in intensity.

Now you can chill for that long, can't you? I'm so proud of you! Well done!

## Notes to Self

### Dementia Sundowning Care Plan

So, your Mom has dementia. And, every evening starting at 5.30, she begins sundowning. She cries. She wants her Mom. She wants to go home. She's inconsolable. She weeps. She wails. She paces. She wrings her hands.

Or maybe it's your Dad. He wants to go home too. But he gets mad about it. He rants. He rages. He wants to go to work. To school. To war. He berates you. Harangues you.

Sundowning is transitional for people with dementia, but can be wrenching for their caregivers. Caregivers feel wrung out long after it's over for the person with dementia. That's why it's so important to have a care plan.

Sundowning is a universal phenomenon, not confined to those with dementia. At close of day, it seems that emotional feelings intensify. Babies get fretful, people feel their loneliness most, even birds go flying around energetically. It's a very busy time throughout the whole of nature. So, keep a sense of proportion.

Each person has sundowning his or her own way because it comes from the content of people's own lives. What we might call normal sundowning does not become violent, crazed or last all night long.

That would be a signal for expert psychiatric intervention , for possible PTSD, undiagnosed schizophrenia or some other serious mental illness or emotional trauma issues.

Normal sundowning typically lasts about a couple of hours. It involves intense feelings of loss, anger, longing, unhappiness, with agitated or anxious behaviors, often repeating the same thing over and over.

Typical might be:

"I have to go home now."

"Is my mother coming?"

"It's time for work."

"Nobody knows where I am."

Pay close attention , because they express real emotions. Your support helps genuine emotional issues, but your planning is needed for sundowning. Before you plan, observe. When does it start? When does it finish? What helps?

Since we don't truly know what sundowning is, we take a multi-aspected approach. Assume hunger and thirst are issues. Assume redirection could help. Assume emotional support, not suppression, is needed. Don't be afraid. Sundowning doesn't harm anyone—it's just distressing. Don't take on the agitation. This will pass in a given period of time.

The Care Plan:

About an hour before sundowning usually starts, give a nutritious snack and both juice and water;

When it starts, be supportive. Don't argue, do console. Don't say,"Your mother died forty years ago," but "I know you miss your Mom," and then act motherly, even if you're a guy

Have your distraction activity ready—a drive in the car, a favorite movie, a cd of waltzes and you two waltzing, an old family photo album, consolation and Kleenex;

Relax and breathe deep, don't get swept up into agitation and do not think it's all due to failed brain cells. That's abandonment of the worst kind. Feelings are real, sundowning temporary. Pay attention to the emotional issues and resolve to work with them. For example, if Dad wants to work, give him chores or gardening to do, so he can feel less useless. If Mom misses her mother so much, be more motherly to your Mom.

That way, you may heal a wound she's always had until now. It takes planning, yes, but you'll be glad you did it.

You can eliminate sundowning with good all-round care plan.

*Notes to Self*
_____

## Understanding Dementia Sundowning

Many people with dementia undergo a regular period of late-afternoon agitation and emotional upset called sundowning. Typically, sundowning starts at a regular time, varying for each individual.

Your aunt may begin showing tearful agitation at around 4pm that may taper off around 6pm. This is her regular pattern.

Your father, on the other hand, may start becoming restless and irritable around 2pm, continuing to about 5pm. While most people seem to start sundowning in the late afternoon, a few start earlier in the day. After breakfast, before lunch—all of this is still usually called sundowning, because it's a regular patterned period of agitation and upset. As caregivers, assume that any such regular period of emotional upset with a limited time span is probably sundowning.

And that you can learn to handle it.

What if you're caring for someone with a radically different pattern? Maybe rampaging around the house all night long, hiding terrified inside closets because someone's going to hurt them, having wildly disturbing nightmares that cause panic attacks, piling up furniture against doors to keep everyone out, smashing things throughout the night. What then?

Then, you MUST seek psychiatric expertise for guidance in knowing what's going on and what to do to help your person. Don't pretend it's normal or there's nothing really wrong. That way, no-one gets helped, including your person.

Those behaviors may indicate untreated PTSD, after-affects of sexual abuse in childhood, undiagnosed serious mental illness such as schizophrenia or psychotic breakdown, other serious mental disturbance or neurological damage of some kind.

Or even something as ordinary as a change of medication or a UTI —both medical side effects or allergic reaction— and Urinary Tract Infections can cause the sudden and unexpected appearance of extremely agitated behavior.

Behavior control of normal everyday dementia through heavy anti-psychotic meds is seldom necessary. Also, we now know that inappropriate use of anti-psychotics on elders kills them. Besides which, most of the usual behaviors of dementia can be managed without extreme measures, when we caregivers learn how to do that.

However, when extreme anxiety, schizophrenic ideation, PTSD after-effects are the real issue, then we need to seek the effective ways that our family members may find peace from their own inner torment. And so we can give them the care they need or even find them the place they need to be in to get that care.

People with dementia who have sundowning behaviors are generally okay if we are okay. Agitation can be very contagious and unskilled, or emotionally troubled, caregivers easily become as agitated as the person they're supposed to be caring for. Most often, as far as I observe in my own working life and my fifteen years as a caregiver support group facilitator, caregiver inability to deal with normal sundowning is closely related to two issues. One is that they over-identify with the transient emotional state. Two is that they have an uneasy relationship with the parent or spouse, which pre-existed the dementia.

Most people can learn how to deal with normal sundowning and I'll bet you can too.

First, learn the pattern in your person. When does it typically start, how long does it last, what are the usual kinds of issues the person talks about? Remember, the sundowning itself is merely a pattern. The issues are very personal and real, often related to loss of role, purpose and place in life.

For example, women express that they are needed at home

to look after their children. Men may want to know where their mothers are or to go to work. Both often want to go home to the place of their childhood, but the actual themes are as varied as people are. Listen carefully, interpret heart-fully, then you'll know what this person needs.

Most people seem to mourn their loss of meaningful life. They seek security and love. They want Mother. They want to go home. They want their important life role back. They feel useless, alone, frightened.

Your dementia care plan must include all these factors. And one more thing—remind yourself that sundowning passes.

## Notes to Self

## Dementia Sundowning

Well, let's start with the easy part. We have no idea what causes sundowning. There's no official reason, only a bunch of guesses.

So, here are mine. Obvious guess: the gradual loss of daylight may cause an internal sense of loss, terror or dysfunction that raises fearfulness. The timing of sundown is also the moment when most people traditionally have been involved in the return to home, the caring for family, the steadying domestic routines. That may be another reason why people become agitated and upset at this time. Emotionally, though not necessarily rationally, they deeply feel their losses.

Remember, this is also the time when fractious babies grow even more fractious, when depressed people become even more depressed. So there may well be an electro-magnetic change in the atmosphere once the sun sets, a change deeper than only the loss of light. Perhaps it affects humans and their moods or sense of safety. We really don't know for sure, but all guesses are valid. Not that all sundowning starts at sundown exactly, of course. It varies from person to person. Some people begin around 2pm, others at other times, but we tend to see most of the agitation changes sometime between 3-ish to 7-ish, with the norm for people with dementia being around 2 hours' duration.

Some caregivers says their person is more upset in the morning, or at lunch time. Despite the name we have given this phenomenon, sundowning occurs at different times for each person. But individuals tend to have a regular time pattern which recurs daily. And the nature of their sundowning is not meaningless, either. For me, one of the most compelling aspects of sundowning is that in that agitation we nevertheless find some essential truths emerging from the person.

We'll hear about real emotions and concerns that have relevance, even if it comes from the past. We hear that they mourn the absence of their parents. They long for the security of that long-ago childhood home. For that life long ago, with family, siblings, friends. Old fears and terrors rise up in them as just a cascade of emotion which sweeps them away for a while. Patterns usually emerge in their behaviors and feelings at these times.

The first person with Alzheimer's I ever looked after began her sundowning promptly at four pm. She stood up in her home of 25 years and announced, "I am going home now," and off she went out of the front door.

That was her routine. The most interesting thing, to me, happened when I asked her, on each occasion, where home was. Each time, it was a different place but they all had the same deep significance. Her parents' house in Dresden, her husband's house in Arkansas, her son's house in Chicago.

I understood she was in search of deep connection, now lost to her. I didn't quite know what this meant, but I knew it meant something. I thought about that for a long time. Then, another woman I looked after later on asked me each evening at 5.30 , "When are my parents coming home to dinner?"

She was 88 at the time, so you can guess the logical answer to that, if I were to give it. Which I never did. Moreover I knew by then that she had lived with her parents all her life, though she was also a professional working woman.

So, once they had died and she developed dementia, she had a deeply ingrained habit of expecting dinner with her parents. It represented everything that gave her emotional security. She needed to have it. And she also could not.

It's a typical dementia dilemma—to deeply and uncontrollably want what no longer exists, other than in the heart. This is the central part of most of the distress expressed in sundowning.

And we can't argue it away, because dementia makes it almost impossible for a person to understand logical explanations. It's not stubbornness or resistence, it is the central wound of dementia. It devastates logical thinking abilities, along with rational arguing abilities.

If you try to argue and logically prove your point—"This is 2011 and your Mom and Dad died 50 years ago, so you can't visit them." —you light up their despair into a raging fire. So, don't do that, okay?

Another woman gave me the clearest example ever of what sundowning was about. It was in a large Memory Care facility in California, where I was a staff trainer. I watched a newly-arrived old Italian woman insisting that she had to go and catch a bus. Staff tried to argue her out of this and she said she had to cook dinner for her little boys.

She was 91 and the little boys were now in their 70s. She insisted. The staff showed her a calendar, a newspaper, her own medical records, all to demonstrate that she was wrong. She was too old to have little sons. They were too old to need her cooked meals. They had wives to cook for them now.

Finally, she stood there, a tiny plump woman with a huge pouter pigeon bosom, confronting them. She patted her capacious bosom and said with dignity, "I see what you're telling me. I know that you're right, but I can only tell you that in here —" as she patted the region of her heart—" I have two little boys who need me."

And she turned, went to her room, sat on her bed and wept. She wanted, they all want, the life in which they had mattered to people they loved.

A life in which commitment and purpose was clear. A life that made sense. Not this strange empty overcrowded meaningless world of dementia in which they found themselves lost.

The themes of sundowning are almost always about attachment versus loss. People, in the midst of agitation, nevertheless express real and relevant issues which are hurting them. These are not rationally thought-out issues. They are needs which burst from the heart.

I understand that many people simply don't want to believe this. Sometimes, family members prefer and even insist that there is no sense in dementia. They are really claiming that this is no longer a real person with real issues. It is as if, having already lost this person as they once knew them, they are rejecting knowing the truth of that person's losses.

They would prefer that this person was empty. Yet, interestingly enough, it is in assuming that there is meaningful process going on emotionally that we can bring answers to the person who is sundowning. Not rational answers, but care answers that work. And we can bring such answers to ourselves.

This person you care for is NEVER an empty, gone-away person. This is someone who lives, longs for and needs. This is someone to whom love still matters. Even though we feel sadness for the expressed pain and longing, we ourselves can BE that love which still matters. That means, we are necessary and needed by them.

It doesn't matter that they call us Mom, when we are their daughters. We make too much of that kind of misnaming— which is only a dementia-memory thing. We would not feel so bereft of who this person was, if we ourselves could become the person they needed. If we could give our mother or father with dementia our moments of whole-hearted love, we too would be healed of many of the pains that their dementia brings us.

Our healing of that pain starts with behaving as if their dementia is not all about us. Perhaps it's all about them. And perhaps our mutual sense of loss, different roots and yet very similar feelings, could be the bridge that brings us to stand beside each other again.

Don't believe me. Try it out. Try to prove me wrong.

209

## A Sundowning Care Plan

**M**ore sleep needed: Encourage your person to sleep longer in the morning and even take a little nap after lunch. This is because most people with dementia are exhausted much of the time. It is very hard to work have dementia and people need more downtime than they are probably getting. When overall exhaustion is reduced, behaviors often become more manageable - think of the overtired infant's acting out behaviors.

**More food and drink needed:**

About an hour before the regular sundowning begins (and most sundowners ARE fairly regular about their performance), give a good little nutritious snack and both water and juice drinks. Because part of the issue may also be hunger and dehydration.

**Lavender needed:**

Start aroma therapy in the afternoon—using pure lavender oil in a diffuser. Lavender has been medically documented to help reduce stress, bring calmness and even improve sleep in everyone, including those with dementia. I've often recommended its use to care facilities and they've reported an almost immediate improvement in stress behaviors.

**Activity plan needed:**

Make a plan for something that will reassure, divert or comfort your person during the sundowning time. This could be a drive in the car, followed by an eating treat of some kind. Watching a favorite DVD, going out for a walk together, sitting close on a sofa and spending quiet social time together.

Empathy needed:

It's also okay to listen to what it said and validate it in an empathetic way. If someone says, "where's my mother?" you can say, " I'm sorry you're really missing her now."

**No arguing needed:**

We can never "argue" a person with dementia out of an emotional reaction because dementia itself takes away the power to be rational. Much more effective is to be sympathetic to the feelings, supportive and kind and then try gently to divert or redirect attention away from the feelings of distress.

**Grieving needed:**

Finally, although we may find it uncomfortable or distressing to see someone we care for be tearful or unhappy, it can be very comforting for that person to actually be allowed to grieve for the losses of a life with dementia.

Many family members are unwilling to do this. As caring people, they really want to "fix" things but we can't fix someone else's Alzheimer's - yet anyway. So the very best thing we can do sometimes is to stand by that person. Or to sit by them. To be kind and accepting and pass the tissues for those tears. That is often the finest and most helpful thing we can do in the presence of someone else's sorrow. And if it touches your own sorrow and you weep too, that's really okay. Shared sorrow can be a very bonding experience.

**Calmness needed:**

Also, know that all agitation passes, but while it's there it's very contagious for caregivers too.

Someone else's distress can make us feel desperate to fix that person. Then we too become agitated and distressed. Try to stay calm, breathe slowly and deeply, make physical contact and sit it out together with the person until it passes, if there's nothing that is working on a particular day.

That is giving another person the gift of our caring presence and it's one of the best things to give to someone with dementia. Also one of the hardest.

If you look after someone who is agitated and upset all night long, for example, I'd urge you to seek help from a psychiatrist to assess whether there are other issues at work. For example, women who have been sexually abused as children may have night terrors. Retired veterans may have post traumatic stress disorder (PTSD).

Other people may have other dominant mental health conditions, as well as, or instead of, dementia. Many families in the past either ignored obvious signs of mental illness in a family member or genuinely did not realize what was going on. Actually, many families still tend to behave this way about the lifelong mental illness of a parent.

Just know that there is an expert out there who knows how to help you. If you're going to take this path, make a careful and impersonal list of observed behaviors in your person.

For example:

212

"Has night fears, heavy use of painkillers, says people are breaking into the house," would be a good start. Don't be tempted to write yourself into that, as in "Keeps me awake all night long, has been addicted to painkillers all her life, is generally nuts," okay? Even if you don't know that something is a symptom, still observe it.

Show your own ability to observe clearly, leave out your anger and let it be all about your person. Why? Because a) you don't want the psychiatrist to think you're the problem, do you? And b) to show clearly the picture of dysfunction, so that c) you really do get the best use of the psychiatrist's time and skills.

And it really can help miraculously. A terrified haunted woman profoundly wounded by childhood abuse and always emotionally on the run can become calm, funny, quirky and kind and the kind of mother you wish she'd always been.

And I find that family healing can really begin when everyone understands that mental health issues, not meanness or indifference, were the real issues in a parent's neglect or rage or abandonment of children. Truth really does set us free.

*Now You're Ready To Speak Dementia*

### Developing Your Dementia Communication Style

Never talk down to people with dementia. They didn't lose their intelligence and they didn't become children. More over, they may well have become more emotionally sharp. Many become more able to pick up underlying emotional communication. So, even though you didn't say it, they know if you're angry, impatient or unhappy.

They have brain injury resulting from the physical depredation on the tissues of the brain. Other perceptive areas may well remain unbroken—heart, feelings, spirit, sensitivity.

So, you need to grow your own capacity to communicate in ways that work with dementia. As caregivers, our job is to find comfortable communication styles that help grow our relationship with the person who has dementia.

**Five First Steps in Speaking Dementia**
**Keep it simple:**

Typically, dementia makes it hard for a person to track complex information. So present information one step at a time. Giving a list of facts or requests or questions make it difficult for memory-impaired people to understand what's going on. Then that may make them upset, confused, angry or resistant;

**Introduce yourself:**

Whether it's your Mom, someone you look after or a resident in long-term care, introduce yourself every time. It feels weird, especially if it's your Mom, but it's easy to do.

"Hey, Mom, it's me, your daughter Janie."

If Mom knows, she'll tell you. If she didn't recognize you, it's a relief for you to do it.

If it's someone you visit or do activities with, don't subject them to test questions like "Do you remember me, Violet?" Just get on and introduce yourself again, for goodness' sake.

**Ask permission:**

You know your person, or maybe you don't if you work in a care facility. However, your person may or may not know you. Don't intrude on their privacy without asking permission.

That's the major cause of violent reaction, when a stranger—that's you—starts being over-personal and physically invasive.

Ask, as in "George, I'm Anna and I'm going to help you with anything you need today. Would it be okay if I helped you get dressed now?"

**Apologize:**

If you do anything to upset your person, apologize. Even if you didn't do anything wrong but you did something that alarmed that person, apologize.

Why? Because it's a great stress management tool. It shows you respect their feelings. It shows you noticed how they were feeling about something you did. It shows you are a safe person for them and you can be trusted.

Since dementia makes it hard for people to trust, having little reliable short-term memory, the more you act like a trustworthy person, the better they feel. The better they feel, the easier everything becomes.

**Back Off:**

If your person gets upset, step back and allow a safe space between you. This rule applies at home and in care facilities.

Usually, if a family member gets upset, we move in closer so we can comfort them. In dementia, we need to move back so they can feel safe.

Only when they feel safe again—get calm, relax, stop raging, cease to cry—can we move towards them. Even then, it's good to ask them if it's okay.

**Five Ways to Create Security:**

**Be At The Same Level:**

215

Standing over someone can be experienced as very threatening. Put yourself at the same level or even lower.

Get a chair and sit with your person before you continue speaking. Better yet, kneel and look up into their face. They might think you're weird, though probably not, but they won't feel threatened.

**Slow Down:**

Slow down in both movement and speech. This allows your person time to process information and communication. It also signals that you are not impatient, not pushing and not demanding. This helps everyone feel safer. Safer is good.

**Offer Limited Choices:**

Giving people choices empowers them, but in dementia you need to limit the choices to something easy. Otherwise, it becomes confusing.

So, for example, you can hold up two sweaters and ask which one the person wants to wear —that's easy. Always show the choices if you can.

If possible, the choice should always be something that can be seen.

"Would you like to go for a walk?" you ask, pointing out of the window or towards the door.

Abstract memory-based choices might be too hard for your person to process.

**Show Patience:**

Trying to hurry a person with dementia can be disastrous —causing panic, extreme slowdown, confusion, anger and agitation in response.

So, take a deep breath, and take the time it needs.

This means, if you have an appointment planned, you allow lots of extra time—just in case.

**Always Let People Teach You:**

Remember, a lot of what we have to learn, our people will teach us through response to our own behavior and requirements. Pay attention to those teachings and be thankful for them.

216

If something didn't work out, take a few deep breaths and relax. Remember, the blessing of dementia is the same as the curse—people forget. They forget your name, but they also forget your stupidity, your bad moods and what failed to work.

Really, people with dementia are often our great spiritual teachers, because they show us that about ourselves we didn't want to see. But they also respond to who we really are, without judgment.

Looking after people with dementia, means we get a fresh start every day. I love that about them.

## Notes to Self

## PATTERN DIALOGUES: HOW TO SAY WHAT YOU SAY

This is a series of possible situations, with possible ways for a caregiver to behave and speak which may lead to more positive outcomes, rather than triggering a negative, emotional or just unhelpful response.

Obviously, these are not necessarily exactly what you'd say. The idea is to see how we can communicate in ways which reduce stress, for both parties, and which reach the person with dementia. Make up your own version, as long as you always accept and work gently with the limitations caused by dementia.

Know you will NEVER be able to assume someone's dementia is not an obstacle to mutual understanding. Just accept it and move round it. Don't punish it.

Each of these situations occurs very commonly among people with dementia and we can turn them into a struggle, a quarrel or a threat, by simply misunderstanding them or by choosing to handle them in a way that causes distress, fear or confusion. Often, our problems as caregivers arise from our own failure to accept where our person actually is in dementia, and also our failure to understand dementia itself.

No criticism intended there. Obviously, as reasonably sane people, we don't want to make our own caregiving even harder. It just takes a while to learn how dementia actually is and what it does to someone we once knew as a very different kind of a person. Or, in the case of care staff, a person we never knew before but have to learn now as a person with dementia.

Remember, no two people do dementia in exactly the same way. That's because everyone is an individual with a separate life history, different needs and varied personalities. That said, there are still dementia issues common to most people with dementia. Short-term memory failure, rational thinking loss, ability to figure things out, reduced or lost.

Your Spoken Attitude:

People with dementia are commonly easily lost and confused inside the limitations of their illness. It's important for you, therefore, to develop speech attitudes which demonstrate kindness and patience. Use a kind tone of voice, not an abrupt one, which may cause your person to feel fear or anger. Even though you have to make allowances for dementia, never speak down to your person.

However, do make your speaking simple and straightforward. That encourages relaxed listening in your person, enables easier comprehension and doesn't lead to confusion.

Many people with dementia lose their ability to process metaphor, which turns a figure of speech into something incomprehensible for them.

Examples:

You: "Why, Mildred, there you are—looking as snug as a bug in a rug!"

Mildred: "A bug? Where?"

Pay attention to your person's response to what you say , because you'll soon notice what they didn't understand. Don't bother to explain —that just makes things worse. Instead, just find a more simple way to express yourself.

Allow a few moments to elapse before trying a different explanation. Also, ask yourself sometimes, "Is this even necessary?" We are normally used to talk which goes back and forth between two people. We expect to consult others. We want to talk over plans and make decisions. All of that is fine, but it may not always apply in your life with a person with dementia.

Are Explanations Necessary?

In dementia, explanations may not always be necessary. In normal life, it's rude to do things without asking or telling anything about the trip. In dementia, this may not be so true.

For example, if you don't want the answer "No!", then don't ask the question. A smart caregiver develops skills of persuasion, avoidance, manipulation and bribery, just as a good mother does. Although those words are often bad words, in helping and handling a person with dementia to get necessary things done, they can be very good words.

So, don't ask, "Are you ready to go to the doctor?"
Instead, just allow plenty of time to get ready, help your person be dressed appropriately and take them off for a drive. Usually no explanation is necessary.

Often, you'll find that the dementia person doesn't ask the normal things the rest of us would. That person often won't question you, want information, find it strange to have been told nothing.

That's not really because of not caring. It's partly because of the daily experience of not remembering. They don't expect to remember. They probably assume they forgot.

In the interests of daily achievement, I think it's okay to be the kind of caregiver who's manipulative, bribing, avoiding and evasive —as long as essentially you are being morally honest in your caring.

It's simply a style of communication that works. Here's an example.

"Let's go for a drive—it's a great day," might achieve much more than asking your Mom if she's ready to go to the doctor. Suppose she says firmly, "No!" to the doctor's visit.. What would you do next? Argue? Reason with her? Insist? All notable failures with dementia people.

Once you'd both upset each other with the ensuring struggle of will, what would you have achieved? Much better to suggest going for a drive. It's evasive, but that isn't bad. It's certainly better than starting a conversation that may become upsetting and unwelcome to you both.

I'm talking about this issue because it is one of the central struggles in dementia between the person who has it and well-meaning caregivers. It causes most problems in families. And good families, at that. Families who really care about their mother, father, spouse and want to treat them with the same respect as before. The respect indeed should be the same as before. The communication style often needs to change.

The person with dementia has become changed and, as caregivers, we have become those who have to take up the slack. Daily battles which achieve nothing will be exhausting, frustrating and pointless.

Once a person has become somewhat or greatly changed by dementia, we honor them best by ensuring their care meets their needs and being kind in our care and our communications.

It isn't a bad thing to move into a communication style which works with dementia. Talk to any mother of young children, any teacher of young children. They develop management styles which work.

As caregivers we have to do the same. It's a constant struggle for us to adjust to the needs and capacities of those we care for. Often, family members find it hard. They may stay in denial for months or even years.

Changing the way we communicate is part of the adjustment we make.

## Notes to Self

### SHOWER DIALOGUES:

You: Okay, Mom, would you like to have your shower now? Mom: I already had a shower today. You: No, Mom, you didn't. Mom: I did!

Now she's angry and you're getting that way. Do not turn this into a power struggle. Caregivers never win those if they go against the wishes of those they care for.

Fear of the Shower

Taking showers is a very big issue for people with dementia. They are frequently experienced as frightening and surprising events. Showers may provoke hitting out in panic or emotional meltdown with weeping and wailing.

Why? No one knows for sure. It may be just too over-whelming. It may be a terrible surprise for someone who forgot water would pour down on them. Or, it may be that the beating of water on the head provokes adverse brain wave or emotional response. Increasingly I lean towards this idea.

Actually, it also doesn't matter why. Our issue is—how? How do we get our person nice and clean? Well, firstly, no old person needs a daily shower. It's bad for frail skin and it can be too exhausting.

Therefore, a couple of wash-cloths, a basin of warm water and clear directions should be your tools at least three days a week. This gives you an ideal alternative on the days when, despite your skills, you can't seem to persuade or inveigle your person into a shower. And it's really okay. People could go without showers their whole life long and still be able to be clean, so let's keep calm about all this. Okay?

**That no-shower today** dialogue goes easily
You: Here, Mom, I've got a nice warm wash-cloth ready here.
Why don't you wash between here and over there? (Pointing to
crotch and behind). That's terrific. Okay, let me get some clean
water and here's a fresh wash cloth. Here, maybe give your face a
good wash, That's good. And now under your arms. Yes! Great.
On shower days, you use a hand-held shower, NEVER an
overhead shower. And you might begin something like this.
You: Let's get you in to have a nice shower, Mom. It's been so
hot, I'll bet you'll feel great when that water gets on you. Here,
let me help you undress. That's great. Now you just get really
comfortable on that shower chair right there and I'll do the rest.
In that chatter, there was not one question.

In dementia care, NEVER ask a question if you don't want
the answer "No!" Instead, make suggestions, keep chattering in
a friendly way (which is not frightening, and is usually
experienced as soothing or at least as a distraction). And, as
much as people make fun of the medical "How are we today,
Mrs M?" it actually serves a socially-unifying purpose in dementia care. It signals that "we" are both on the same side.

Once Mom or Dad, or your person, is seated in a good
shower chair (not a stool), you begin using the handheld
shower starting from the feet. Work your way up, taking
longer where you need to, and you stop at the neck before
using the shower on the face . That depends on your person.

There's no need to be spraying water on the head and face
in an old person's shower time, especially when it's someone
with dementia. And I'd suggest you don't get the hair wet either.
That's best done by a hairdresser, unless you know that your
person is okay with it.

Some progressive care places are now using a different approach to the I-giver-you-shower scenario. They have care staff
go right into the shower with the resident and they report that

223

this approach works very well. It changes the whole dominance issue, which is what scares residents, into "we have a shower."

I love that innovative approach and you could do that at home too.

## *Notes to Self*

## USING -THE-TOILET DIALOGUES:

Lots of people with dementia become confused about the toilet, how to use it and what to do. Our society has grotesque judgments about toilet issues and old people. Actually, about the whole process of urination and defecation. But that's just us.

And if that's you, just remind yourself how long it takes to get a little kid to learn these skills—an average of about six months. Then it might make more sense to you why people with dementia have forgotten them. They lose the skill because of their declining brain capacity to recall that long-ago learning. They didn't get dirty, they got dementia.

Arm yourself with all the tools of helping an elder with toilet use, and the whole thing will become easier for you.

Believe me, when I started out in caregiving and was confronted with this task, I never thought I'd manage it without disgust, to be honest. It took me days to lose that initial sense of disgust. But I realized my feelings of repulsion were using up extra energy I really couldn't spare and I was able to let go of it. It never has to be your favorite thing to deal with. Just settle for reasonably non-emotional in your attitude. That'll do. And remember, probably your Mom did it for you.

Also, having protective gloves, plenty of toilet paper and wipes, garbage bags at the ready, all makes it easier. We equate helping people with their toilet procedures as them having become totally childish. However, it's not only the old who might need this help. It's also the very ill, the badly injured, the very disabled mentally and or physically—more people than you might think. It's not a judgment situation.

**The Toilet Dialogue:**
**You:** Okay, Mom, let's go visit the bathroom.
**Mom:** I've just been. (Not true, by the way.)
**You:** Well, but you just ate lunch/a snack/that fruit/whatever, so this is probably a good time and it wouldn't hurt a bit to try. Then we could watch Oprah/the golf/Lawrence Welk/make cookies.

Did you notice that you didn't argue a bit? Very good—because that would have been a waste of time. Arguing with a person with dementia is a no win/no win situation. You certainly won't win and your person cannot, because people with dementia can't follow logical argument and, confronted with that, they feel threatened and angry or upset. For them, when you use logical argument, it's as if you are hitting them in the head.

You also used bribery on your Mom—a very good management tool in dementia, together with persuasion and manipulation. Well done!

226

Don't forget, males need to have their penis tucked inside the toilet bowl (if sitting) and females need to be reminded to wipe from front to back to avoid bladder infections. In my experience, all older women with dementia have forgotten that, which is too bad, because they get a lot of urinary tract infections (UTI) but you can still remind them.

You hand out the toilet paper in a generous wad and get them to drop it into the garbage bag you're holding up. Remember, people born in the Depression use only one sheet at a time—not good for hygiene. So, hand them extra.

Many people with dementia gradually become unable to recognize the body feelings that remind them to head for the toilet. They need a regular schedule—about once every one and a half hours is good —and you are the time-keeper for that.

## Toilet Schedule Dialogue:

**You:** Mom, let's try the bathroom visit again now. **Mom:** I don't need to. **You:** Well, you might be right, but we're going out soon and we'd better see about having a pee first. Because you never know.

Notice how you blend you and your Mom as "we". That just helps make it harder for her to resist. I don't know if you're really going out soon, but I can assure you that God forgives little manipulative lies in the interest of dementia well-being.

Other ingenious things to say that we invented were:

The doctor wants you to go to the bathroom more;

You're going to need more room inside to eat/drink.

It might just be worth a try.

Once you start on the road of being more inventive and understand that you can never win a caregiver battle, then you'll find you can win every time—well, okay, almost every time. We caregivers usually get stuck in useless struggle when we feel that we are on one side and our person on the other.

That's hard for both parties. When we can move together to stand on the same side, we find solutions for many things. We can also be less lonely, less beleaguered and less threatened. And, remember, you can always ask your person what he or she thinks, wants or needs.

I'm not saying you'll get an answer that the average person on the street could interpret, but I'll bet you'll get an answer that will help in some way.

## GOING HOME

Going home is a huge theme in dementia and it has a wide variety of momentary meanings, though only one deep meaning.

"I'm going home," said by a determined old lady with dementia, as she heads out of the door at 4pm, can mean any of the following:

1. Going home to Mom and Dad, and the farm, in the 1930s, in the Dakotas;

2. Going home to my first husband's house where we raised our three children;

3. Going home to my most recent abode —which is actually the least likely meaning;

4. Going home to death, God, heaven, to meet my family in the afterlife, to the eternal sleep.

What do you say?

The least useful thing a caregiver can ever say to a person with dementia who wants to go home is the one thing most often said to them: "Oh, but this is your home!"

Wrong. If this felt like home, your person wouldn't be looking for a different one. And absolutely, no-one in a care facility should ever be told it's their home. That's a well-meaning but outrageous denial of the sense of loss that a resident has once he or she is in enforced residence in an institution.

There are a number of ways to explore what people want back when they talk of going home. The obvious way is to ask and then to answer in a respectful way, to acknowledge what's going on. The following are some examples of how to take part in a going home dialogue.

**At Home:**

**You:** Where are you going, Mom?

**Mom:** I'm going home now.

**You:** Oh, can I go with you?

You both go out of the front door together.

**You:** Where are we going, Mom?

**Mom:** Home.

**You:** Okay then. So, who's there? (Where's that? How far is that?)

**Mom:** My parents.

**You:** Oh, I see. Er, your parents?

**Mom:** Yes.

**You:** You're missing them right now, huh?

There are many directions in which to take this conversation, but the rational present-day time line is NOT one of them.

Use your imagination to figure out how Mom feels. She is probably filled with a longing to see her parents. She's lonely and unsure of everything and her long-term memory, still reasonably intact, draws her back to past security. Her feelings are now. Her longing for her parents torments her right now. It is now she needs comfort because she has lost those whom she feels she needs so badly.

As caregivers, we give comfort in the present time, even though the longings may be attached to long-dead people.

Not only is it useless to insist her parents are dead—because she won't believe you—but it avoids the real issue. Her loneliness and sense of loss right now, in the room with you.

Anyway, isn't it true that our parents or other close family are always alive in some sense within us as long as we remember them? We always have our feelings, even if the people in them are dead. So, your Mom who wants her Mom is not really out of line. She's only out of calendar.

You insisting they are dead does nothing to help her deal with that.

She has an emotional need now which someone needs to fulfill. Mom needs a Mom. So this is where a caregiver provides motherly care to this woman.

The same would be true in any care facility. When old people want their mothers, it's a sure sign they feel like motherless children. Going rational on them only makes that feeling worse. Be comforting.

No need to lie. No need to tell the truth. The need is that you fill that empty space within them. That's what you concentrate on.

**Response patterns to the need for mothering:**

Mom indicates she's going home to Mother, that she needs her mother, that it's been a long, long time since she saw Mother.

**You:** I know, I know. I'm so sorry you're upset. You really miss your Mom right now, don't you?

**Mom:** Yes, I do.

Mom weeps. You do what you do for any emotionally distressed human being of any age. You respond with kindness, you listen well, you offer comfort. You become the comforter because it is that comfort she needs, She might want her mother, but she will probably accept your motherliness.

Caregivers who argue with their person have usually panicked, because they know Mom's mother is dead and they don't know what to do. More intuitive caregivers understand that what they do is be motherly —and guys can do that too, by the way. It's not demented for a human being to long for the kind of unconditional love that parents ideally provide.

Soldiers dying in battle cry out for their mothers. Their need is very great. That's also true for the old who weep for their parents. Their tears usually do not go on for long, especially if you offer the right kind of comfort.

Don't try to fix anything. Just be there and be kind. As the emotion begins to settle, then you can get them back into the real life of now.

230

You: Shall we go back now and have some dinner? I've made a really nice meal," and so on.

The great thing about the going-home theme is that it usually has limited broadcasting time. It usually connects with sundowning, though it may not always. There may be other triggers for emotional hunger to see long-dead parents again. Learn the triggers, learn how to be comforting, never use logic to hurt your person and know it will be over —until the next time.

In care facilities, the going-home theme can become much stronger. That's because most care facilities are not very homelike. Often, residents have far too little to do and there may be very little emotional support there. It is still not rare for staff to try using logic and argument with residents who want to go home.

This frustrates the staff and it distresses the resident whose needs are still not being met, so no-one is helped. . Once staff understand the way that memory actually works in dementia, they can be much more helpful. Unskilled caregivers feel they have to "fix" the situation by "making" the resident feel better. However, what helps residents to feel better is to have people respecting how they feel. Again, they need someone to stand beside them, not to be in opposition.

Unskilled staff feel bad if a resident feels bad. A more confident and experienced caregiver understands that people feel how they feel and it's no-one's fault. It's just part of normal life for people to sometimes feel sad and needy, especially in care facilities. What they most need is a listening ear, preferably attached to real emotional intelligence. Someone more skilled in understanding how human emotions work will be able and willing to listen to someone else's sorrow. That person won't be afraid to talk about the issue at hand.

You: You're really missing your Mom right now, aren't you?
Resident: I am. I haven't seen her for so long.
You: She sounds as if she's a great Mom.
Resident: Oh she is, she is, that's why I miss her.

You: So, what's the best thing about your Mom?

And this opens the way for that person to be able to share her experiences with her mother. This evokes for her what it was like to be in the company and care of her mother. This, in turn, re-awakes her sense of being loved by her mother. Being listened to by a sympathetic person also evokes that same sense of being loved. So the conversation and the sympathy put her back in touch with her mother. And, by the way, I would encourage the use of present tense, not to deceive but to honor the present need.

It is very seldom that there is more insistence at that time on seeing the mother. I won't say it never happens, but it does not happen often.

What do you say if someone with dementia demands to know the truth? What happens when an old woman corners you in the kitchen, as happened once to me, and says, "I want you to tell me right now—are my parents alive or not?"

I never lie to people with dementia, although I may evade, avoid and omit inconvenient or unhelpful truths. So, I told her the truth—that they were dead and had been for over twenty years.

It was very distressing for her to hear that. Screaming, crying and slamming doors followed, her not me. She left the house, I followed her. She walked round the block and back into her own house. I sat for ten minutes on the wall outside the house, wondering what on earth to do. Then I knocked on her door.

"Oh, how nice!" she said and invited me in, apparently having forgotten the whole drama.

I understand you won't necessarily ever want to speak like me. You don't have to. Those are all just samples so you can see how someone might speak. And that's actually how I do speak.

All you really need to know is how to avoid conflict, how to understand dementia and how to get the good things you want for your person with dementia.

You are being in that sense, the good parent, the good guide, the helper, the caregiver and you're using communications skills which acknowledge all of those things.

These situations don't always go smoothly. Not going smoothly, however, doesn't seem to take away from the possibility of the one with dementia coming back to a more even and calm emotional state—which is not always true for the caregiver.

Most of these dialogues may show you how to avoid trouble. If they don't, it is usually only you, the caregiver, who will remember the trouble. Dementia allows a person to weep, rage and recover in time for dinner.

I suggest you follow that good example.

## Notes to Self

*Drop That Word Alzheimer's:*
*Thinking About Dementia*

## Is it Even Alzheimer's?

You do know, don't you, that Dr Alzheimer's Alzheimer studies were not studies of old people?

No, my friends and fellow caregivers, the good doctor studied people who had what we would now call **early-onset Alzheimer's,** the appearance of dementia in a person under 55. His landmark case was a woman of 51, who died within a year of him first meeting her. Modern researchers have even suggested that possibly she did not have Alzheimer's but a completely different medical condition

235

So, our modern Alzheimer's is not Dr Alzheimer's Alzheimer's. The good doctor, who died in 1915 at the age of 51, carried out his studies from the end of the 19th century until his death. Then, his studies sort of lay quietly gathering the dust of medical history.

From 1969 onwards, doctors became interested all over again. For one thing, more and more people were old. Women seldom died in childbirth or children in infancy. Brain researchers were looking at the old and asking themselves, what old really looked like. And was dementia in old people a disease?

International drug companies were the big push behind new research interests into human aging. The biggest international conferences on dementia, aging and the brain from 1969 to 1972 were financed by the very drug companies that had made their former fortunes on fighting the plagues and societal killer diseases which seemed to be coming under control in the 1960s and 1970s.

I have been

years now and I have always paid attention to what I see among the elders. Furthermore, in the process of writing care books and giving workshops all over the world, I have had many further opportunities to observe the world of elders and their families dealing with dementia in many countries.

So, this is what I've noticed. The term Alzheimer's seems to be very over-used. In everyday life, it's extremely over-used, because people are terrified of it. That leads me to think there's not as much about as you might fear.

I also noticed from the very first person I ever looked after there was a lot more meaningful stuff going on than family ever acknowledged. It often happens that family members begin to dismiss their elders as viable people once symptoms rule normal functioning. Especially if the family has problems.

To me, the first woman I cared for was an interesting, thoughtful person, with a good sense of humor, very relational and able to talk, interact and tell her own history, in varying degrees of competence from day to day. She had also had an horrendous life of many losses, being a Jewish survivor who fled Nazi Germany.

When I met her, I liked her immediately. I even felt that I kind of knew her, recognized who she was in some way.

As a brand-new Alzheimer's caregiver, I went to seminars and workshops, including some at UC Berkeley. The official attitude towards Alzheimer's was neither useful nor informative, especially adding little useful to my daily routine, and certainly

236

not to understanding and creating relationship with the person I cared for.

In the years since then, in fact, the very word Alzheimer's has come to be malignant with dread and horror. Probably great for fund-raising, but a negative force of darkness in our society. In fact, it has rebounded horribly. So much was, and is, projected onto the very idea of Alzheimer's that caregivers have come to expect the very worst from it.

This has meant that family caregivers have been unable to discern the difference between regular Alzheimer's and the manifestations of PTSD, serious mental illnesses such as schizophrenia, psychosis and bi-polar conditions which need—and often in elders don't get—useful psychiatric intervention.

Now, THAT is a tragedy, for caregivers and for their suffering family members who don't get the help they need. They also don't get the opportunity to come to the peace that may well be possible once they get the right medication for the right condition.

So, all that projection and fear and ignorance has led us into a huge national tragedy. We seem incapable of bringing normal commonsense into our discernment. We have forgotten what regular old age is like. It is a huge public relations nightmare.

Regular aging is an arc of living old. It goes from pretty darn fit and well to regular old age stuff.

Even the healthiest person starts to have Proper Noun memory issues from the mid-50s on. Remembering or learning other people's names, a book or movie title -- normal age-related stuff.

Then from the mid-60s comes the minor daily difficulty of thinking of the word you want to say but it comes to you when you let it go -- normal.

Americans have swallowed wholesale the myth that we need not age and that if we shows signs of decline, that is illness of some kind —preferably the kind that drug companies can spin gigantic amounts of profits from.

I know Americans really want to believe that, if you stay thin enough, eat right enough and exercise long enough, you won't get old. And I know my fellow Americans now well-enough to understand that hidden inside that is an even darker belief—if we're fit, we need never die.

Well, my darlings, that is not true.

We all die. We most of us right now will probably live to be old and in that process, probably stuff will happen that you didn't really want to happen. Tough noogies—that's life.

Let's not be identifying every mild memory decline as pre-Alzheimer's. Let's stop stringing together a long hooked line that says every mild cognitive decline leads to Alzheimer's, because observably it does not. And when it does lead to dementia, very often now it leads to the wrong diagnosis of Alzheimer's.

Terror of Alzheimer's creates huge stress in people who might as well say, "Gosh darn it, my memory isn't what it used to be." And stress, by the way, is really bad for memory process.

I myself through my own unscientific observations have identified a pattern of ten things to be found involved with memory issues in old age, and most of them you already know about. Anything that's normally health-provoking will also raise your protection against memory issues.

Ten things to avoid, identify and repair:

The big issue found in almost everyone who goes on to finally be diagnosed with dementia is to have undergone a stressful childhood and NEVER to have undertaken to deal with that issue to find emotional peace through therapy, spiritual development or anything else.;

Unhealthy physical lifestyles—including addictions, lack of exercise, poor nutritional choices all reduce your chance of health, including brain health;

Untreated mental health conditions including depression and eating disorders which discourage healthy living;

Every surgical procedure using general anesthesia, in a person over 60, makes it more likely that person could develop dementia—due to the anesthesia;

Too much alcohol can lead to Korsakoff's Syndrome, a dementia due to alcohol damage;

Too many medications mixed together cause the appearance of dementia, which is too often called Alzheimer's;

Contaminants in water and food build toxicity in the body which can also cause dementia.    No groundwater in the whole United States is now free of pesticides, medications, hormones and other noxious chemicals. Some people claim they have resolved their dementia through chelation cleansing of the body system;

There are many conditions in which dementia appears, but is fixable.

For example, Normal Pressure Hydrocephalus in which fluid pressure builds up in the brain of an older person and can be reduced to normal, at which time dementia decreases and may even disappear altogether.

. Too many people, said to have Alzheimer's, have never been through the Alzheimer's work up, which is paid for by Medicare;

Dementia is a normal issue in old people dying and is not a disease.

Just as a bonus, I'm going to throw in my observations of what seems to keep elders either dementia free or able to function well with the support of others.

Social interaction;

239

Pets;
   Hip replacements done with epidurals, not general anesthesia;
   Good food which includes, by the way, butter, honey, caffeine,
salt and moderate alcohol, unless your doctor has a darn good
reason why not, other than current medical myth;
      Spiritual practice of some kind;
      Developing gratitude and kindness;
      Reaching beyond the generational gap;
      Sunshine, twice a day for 15 minutes per time;
      Digestive enzymes, which allows your food to feed your brain;
.Interest in news, friends and the world and a rich interior life.

## *Notes to Self*

## Do You Really Know Alzheimer's?

I read the Alzheimer's on-line sites and the caregiver sites a lot. And really, sometimes, I just want to sit down and beat someone over the head with a large medical dictionary.

I live with and care for people with dementia. And I'm very happy to do that. I'm not a medical person and I try to learn what I can. As part of doing that, I read a lot. I also pay attention to the all the people I've know who were diagnosed as having Alzheimer's. I learn and practice and experiment to see what works for those I care for. Because, if it works for them, it'll work for me.

What alarms me is that the medical world itself is amazingly undiscriminating about the term Alzheimer's disease. Too many doctors don't pick up on medication allergies, and specific other conditions. And maybe that wouldn't matter so much except that the real cause might be fixable, adjustable or even curable.

So if a medical doctor has decided, **without the full Alzheimer's** work-up, that your mother has Alzheimer's, she could fail to get the medical care and intervention that might help her real problem. She might have Normal Pressure Hydrocephalus, a brain pressure issue that often begins with walking and balance issues, followed by the onset of dementia. It is much more commonly than previously thought and can be helped and even cured, IF someone checks for it.

We hear a lot these days about the Alzheimer's work-up. This, ironically, is actually the anything-but-Alzheimer's work-up

241

because it seeks out other discernible causes of dementia-like manifestations.

Current forensic studies are now showing that even when an appropriate work-up has been done, the diagnosis of Alzheimer's may be as much as 50 percent erroneous. Scary, huh?

The medical world sold us the term Alzheimer's, claiming initially that most dementia is Alzheimer's and that dementia is an unnatural disease condition.

What makes me unhappy is the undiscriminating use of the term Alzheimer's disease. All of us non-medical people can make some darn good guesses about people's real dementia when we know someone's personal history and their so-called dementia behaviors.

If your Dad drank heavily all his life, that dementia he had was probably NOT Alzheimer's disease but **Korsakoff's Syndrome.**

Your Uncle did not have Alzheimer's disease but had a lengthy **open-heart surgery** which perhaps saved his life but caused cognitive damage to his brain —probably due to anesthesia.

Your spouse did not get Alzheimer's in the hospital—he had **temporary hospital dementia,** or a delirium, which is most often cured by leaving hospital.

Why is it important to use the right term? Well, for one thing, because it's the right term, okay?

Why are medical people identifying dementia wrongly and too often still without actually ordering up an Alzheimer's workup? That's a very good question and your guess is as good as mine. Unfortunately, I suspect that sometimes old age and apparent dementia come up against medical feeling that there's no point in finding out more, due to inner age bigotry.

But there is a point. For one thing, we should know the name of what ails us, if it has a name. If it doesn't have a name, we need to know the cause. Old age is not a diagnosis. So don't settle for that as an answer.

Elders may be normally somewhat forgetful and occasionally confused. That is simply part of the extreme aging process and it doesn't have to be medicalised.

It's a normal part of the arc of aging. The start of dementia in the very old is merely the drop of their immune system as they walk slowly towards the gates of death. It's nothing to be afraid of. It is not insanity. It doesn't need a psychiatrist. It needs you, the person who cares.

We human beings never become people to whom love is unimportant. So, just relax and be kind. That's often the best medicine.

## Notes to Self

## ARE YOU THE BOSS OF MOM AND DAD?

If they clearly aren't managing, then YES, you are. However, as you really know deep down inside, it's not that simple. How much do your aging parents appreciate you raising the subject of them not managing life so well?

Well, let me put in this way. Do you remember how much you enjoyed that sex and virginity talk with Mom when you were fourteen and she was suspicious? That's pretty much how much your parents want you to talk to them about age, health and self-neglect.

244

No-one wants interference from their kids. Certainly no one wants to admit that they aren't aging well. And inevitably, they probably hear criticism in you even raising the topic.

So, that is why you approach this subject gently, kindly and without reproach. And did I mention tact? Oh yes, and taking stuff on yourself. Now some parents are such open people, so self-aware and unafraid of admitting their life circumstances that there will be no problem at all.

"Why, son, we're so glad you mentioned your concerns about us. We were just going to talk to you about what we need and can't do any more."

There's a couple of sentences rarely spoken in the intergenerational talk realm. No, you need lots of soft-soaping here. One reason is that your parents may actually not be fully aware of their loss in function. Two, is that, if they are, they even more don't want to talk about it. The underlying feelings here are how often their shame,and their fear dominate them.

Be very kind and approach this as a way of supporting them, not as proving them incompetent.

Even if they're stubborn, disbelieving and dismissive, don't try to make them wrong. They already are wrong, in a sense, because they can't take care of themselves efficiently. That is why they'll fight you. Since someone has to be the grownup, that would be you and your siblings.

You might want to share your concerns with siblings first. To get a reality check of what you're seeing. Then you could usefully get together to figure out the major concerns and begin making a plan.

Unless your parents are in real danger from their own incompetence, start with a few extra nice inputs into life. Take meals around, have someone help in the house. If they protest, here's a way that often works.

You say some version of "Golly gee, Mom and Dad, I know you say everything is okay, and it probably is, but I just worry about you guys. You've done a lot for me and I want to do things for you now. "

Choose your own words, but emphasize your love, your gratitude for what they gave you and your wish to enable them to have a great style of living without worries as they age..

Why? Because they will only accept your help when they feel safe with you, respected by you and loved by you. Then they know your help is love, and not judgment. They probably prefer to be helped through love. Just as you would. Otherwise, they will fight you all the way.

It's painful, and embarrassing, for an elder not to manage as well as before. Most prefer not to be reminded of it. So, you need to step up beside them, not take an oppositional attitude against them.

You have no idea, until it happens, how badly elders who are failing don't want to be railroaded into care scenarios which are obnoxious to them.

I have met elders who ran away from home, often driving thousands of miles—badly, of course —to get away from bossy kids. At best, their resistence makes happy communication difficult. At worst, they will die alone in a faraway place.

So, be willing to take some time to negotiate in a helpful, friendly way. Offer small things and work your way up, unless they are in imminent peril. Make this an extended, continuing, friendly conversation, taking it one step at a time.

If you and your siblings can't work out a successful and agreeable plan, think abut bringing a mediator in to help. An outsider often sees more of the game on both sides and has an outsider's view.

If no middle way can be found, then it's possible a whole family intervention must happen in which solutions are put into effect even against your parents' wishes. This isn't always bad. Many elders live in failing situations, where they have become isolated, lonely, unable to manage in a steadily declining lifestyle.

Moving into the right kind of communal housing can bring such elders a whole new lease on life, in a way they never thought possible.

So keep trying to help them work things out and remain always on their side, however annoying they may be. If serious dementia issues are present, just get in there to save that life to live for a better, safer and more fulfilling day.

## *Notes to Self*

## Is Alzheimer's the Most Common Dementia?

What I'm sharing with you here is the bemusement of any caregiver who also reads about dementia and collects people's histories of their own family caregiving involvement with trying to get through the dementia maze.

I'm a caregiver and you'd be amazed how often people ask me if something is really Alzheimer's.

And maybe none of this would matter if everyone, especially those with parents  diagnosed with Alzheimer's, were not so scared of the disease. Sadly, people have even killed themselves rather than even risk having the so-called Alzheimer's they thought their parent had.

That's why we must question medical assertions without much backing. It is very important to know that something is definitely, or only maybe, so. Especially a major issue in family and family caregiving life.

Everyone thinks they know Alzheimer's when they see it. What they see, in fact, is a collection of behaviors. They think  it's Alzheimer's. But really, it's a message -- "Help needed here!" Many conditions look like our idea of Alzheimer's. Alzheimer's is only one of many  dementias we're familiar with these days. Even so-called dementia behaviors can be due to other factors entirely. Anything from depression, losses in sight and hearing, other illnesses. All that may look like our idea of Alzheimer's. So, supposing your mother,  was showing a bundle of the de-mentia-like behaviors.  What do you do?

You take her for the complete Alzheimer's work-up. Finally,

the diagnosis is "a dementia of the Alzheimer's type", written in her medical record as DAT.

Sounds definite, doesn't it. But, as yet, there is no definitive marker that confirms Alzheimer's. It's a default diagnosis.

If I were to interpret that phrase, "dementia of the Alzheimer's type", its meaning is more like "Looks like Alzheimer's, so I guess it is Alzheimer's."

Now, if I had foot fungus, I'd put up with that "looks like" as a diagnosis. But if my family is dealing with dementia, I'd want something better. Because, if that was my family, we'd would all be in pain.

By the way, as a longterm caregiver, I've seen plenty of people still able to be happy, to feel love and to have a darn good time on an Alzheimer's day. That isn't usually how families look at it and I certainly don't blame them. I do understand. I just don't share their dread.

**248**

Some dementias can be identified with certainty—vascular dementia, multi-infarct dementia, dementia due to insufficient oxygen to the brain and so on. That's because actual physical evidence and signs of damage can be identified in CAT scans or MRIs or oxygen measurement, and so on. Sometimes lifestyle may identify a dementia, as in alcoholism and the dementia of Korsakoff's Syndrome. But right now, we have no indicator that means, yes, this IS Alzheimer's and no other dementia. Plus, just because Alzheimer's is the most often-used term, doesn't make it in reality the main dementia of our time.

Right now, as a non-medical follower of the dementia trail for the past 20 years, it seems as if the term is rather loosely-used. And it will be until we can definitively identify Alzheimer's.

So, no, I doubt Alzheimer's actually is the most-common dementia of our time.

## Alzheimer's Or Not?

U ncle Fred has Alzheimer's. Mrs Morales has Alzheimer's.
Your grandmother has Alzheimer's. Bill the Mailman has
Alzheimer's. You know because you saw it. Memory problems,
confusion, can't follow a conversation, dropping things and getting
upset—you know Alzheimer's when you see it, right? Well, far
be it from me to say nyah-nyah-nyah-nyah-nyah, so I'll just say
"Wrong!"

Now I'm no medical expert. So I'm not diagnosing here. You
have the benefit of my 20 years of being educated by people who
seemed to have Alzheimer's. And some of them did. A lot of
them did. But many did not.

Take your Uncle Fred, for example. He's 77 and his wife died
a year ago and his problem might be loneliness, isolation and
grief which is turning into depression.

Mrs Morales has Normal Pressure Hydrocephalus. You know,
what her grandma would have called "water on the brain". It's
much more common than anyone realized before and it can develop as an aging condition as the natural drainage of fluid from
the brain becomes obstructed. This often shows up first as walking and balance problems, with dementia following.

Bill-the-Mailman actually has Korsakoff's Syndrome, seen in
over-dedicated drinkers with a long history of alcohol abuse.
But you're right about Grandma. She has Alzheimer's disease.
You and I, when we look at each of these people, see our idea of
Alzheimer's. And it's not that our idea is wrong.

It's that what looks like Alzheimer's also looks like many other
conditions. Lots of things look like Alzheimer's because we our-

selves don't know the difference. And, even if we did know the difference, the only way to confirm a diagnosis is after all the testing has been done.

Because even though there is a lot of Alzheimer's around—according to our current state of medical knowledge—there's also a lot of the other stuff too. Named dementias, of which Alzheimer's is only one. Dementias without names but associated with health conditions.

Apparent dementias which are really side effects of prescribed medications. Or lack of certain vital vitamins. Or a bladder infection. Or allergic reactions. Or mental illness. Or PTSD.
At one seminar I attended at UC Berkeley, the doctor presenting it told us there were 50 to 60 dementias of old age. And that's separate from the not-dementias which only look like dementias but are actually something else.

So, you see, it's really no wonder that we scarcely know our Alzheimer's from our Korsakoff's. It's not that we're ignorant. It's just that mere observers can't diagnose, even if—and this part really is important—they are doctors.

Without that all-important Alzheimer's work-up, which these days should absolutely include a brain pressure test, we don't know what we're dealing with. So, don't make guesses. Don't let doctors make guesses or say, "At her age..." as if being old had to mean being less than well. Get the work-up done. The full work-up. Not that little in-office Mini-Mental test.

Many people ,who look as if they have dementia, do not. Of the people who do, anything from 15 to 20 percent have treatable even fixable conditions. And, bottom line, even if someone has Alzheimer's disease, don't you think you need to know?

I do.

## ALZHEIMER'S VS DEMENTIA

I'm always amazed to find that the most common question I get asked during workshops is still, "What is the difference between Alzheimer's and dementia?"

Alzheimer's disease **is** a dementia, one of many. Especially, the many dementias of old age. Some have specific names, many don't. Among the dementias with names are Alzheimer's disease, Korsakoff's Syndrome which is a Vitamin B deficiency connected with alcohol abuse, vascular dementia, AIDS dementia, Lewy Body disease and many more.

**All Alzheimer's disease is dementia, but not all dementias are Alzheimer's.**

There are also dementias associated with other health conditions, but without their own special name. Such as, lack of sufficient oxygen to the brain, Normal Pressure Hydrocephalus and dementia of the dying process.

There are temporary dementias, such as when an elder goes into hospital. It is quite common for someone to develop what looks like dementia but which tends to gradually clear up after returning home again. This is actually called a delirium, the term for a temporary dementia.

The term dementia really only describes what we see. It is a syndrome of behaviors, brain function loss and memory issues that we see affecting a person.

Dementia does not describe only memory issues. It also includes confusion, problems with rational thinking, cognitive decline.

There are a lot of normal age-related memory issues which are not dementia—trouble remembering names, the title of a movie and so on. When we see multiple dysfunctions affecting normal life, that's when we get our person to the doctor for a full Alzheimer's investigation.

By the way, Dr Alzheimer's Alzheimer's disease is not really our Alzheimer's. Back in the early years of last century, the good doctor Alzheimer researched what was then called "Pre-senile dementia"—what we now call early-onset dementia.

He did not investigate dementias in elders, the most common dementia we hear spoken about today. Now, whether Alzheimer's is really the most common dementia in reality—well, that is quite another question.

That is actually a bit of a mystery. Well, a big mystery. There is so far no actual marker for Alzheimer's. There is no genetic marker, no chemical marker, even the physical deterioration is not absolutely Alzheimer's beyond all doubt. New studies reveal that possibly as many of 50 percent of those diagnosed as having Alzheimer's do not have the brain deterioration considered to be the evidence of Alzheimer's —those infamous plaques and tangles. This of course is only established after death, on autopsy. This will perhaps change as research continues into this most-researched of all medical conditions.

A lot of people don't realize an official diagnosis of Alzheimer's is actually a default diagnosis. It is what remains after other identifiable medical issues have been eliminated—medication issues, liver problems, strokes, cancer and so on. To me, a very non-medical person, it seems like saying someone has a cold but not knowing which virus caused it. But hey, as long as they continue the search for the cure of the common cold—or, in this case, Alzheimer's—I guess that's okay for the moment.

So, just tell your friends, all Alzheimer's is dementia but not all dementia is Alzheimer's. And what you guess is dementia may not be dementia at all.

So, be kind to each other.

## Notes to Self

## QUESTION EVERYTHING

This is the most important thing I want to end this book with. You, as the caregiver, are the on-the-spot expert.

You may lack medical expertise and be inexperienced about dementia, but you know your person. And, alas, let me tell you, when it comes to what everyone knows about dementia, you'd be surprised how little people sometimes know and that may even include doctors.

So remember, your feeling that something is wrong, that something new is going on and it might not be good, is almost always valid. And, anyway, so what if you were wrong? Better get your person to a hospital or a doctor to be told officially that you're wrong.

If your person seems different after starting a new medication, and you don't like the differences, get back to the doctor. Most medications are negotiable when bad side effects are going on. Write down the differences you notice and check them out on-line with medication side-effects. Because, that difference you see or feel, may just be the start of an allergic reaction that could kill your person. You are the gate-keeper. So, never be embarrassed to be a nuisance on behalf of your person.

Maybe they're starting a stroke reaction. Maybe they have a urinary tract infection. You don't have to know what is wrong, only that something IS wrong. You don't have to know the answers, only the questions. You may sense when your person is beginning to die. Caregivers know and sense these things. It's not your psychic powers—although it could be—it's that you know your person and you know when something has changed. Most carergivers do.

W hen you need practical medical advice, how to put protective underwear on your person and what kind, you need advice from a nurse. Ask your doctor to arrange for that. Most things like that are covered by Medicare.

If you aren't getting what you need, in the way of medical help or helpful equipment, keep asking until you get it. There's wonderful help out there, especially under Medicare, but you sometimes have to be persistent to get it.

When you think your person may be dying, or approaching that zone, ask your doctor for a Hospice assessment. If your doctor is reluctant—and they often are—insist. Actually, your doctor cannot stand in the way of making such a referral.

And, if Hospice feels that such help is appropriate, it will transform the whole experience. Their job is to be a guide, a comfort and to keep pain away. Hospice support is wonderful and you can call Hospice into a care home or nursing facility too. You will never regret that support.

## Notes to Self

_____

# On-Line Help Resources

Since the greatest amount of easy-to-find information, with continuous updating, is to be found on the internet, this is a basic guide to the vast knowledge of the internet that awaits you.

If you don't have a computer, your local library will and there will also be willing people there to teach you how to use it. If you really can't or won't do that, then ask a young relative, or a kind neighbor, to find the information you need and print it out for you.

These days, however old you are, I promise there are people much older getting into useful relationships with information on the internet. There is nothing as useful easily available, so I urge all caregivers to take that step forward.

The Dementias:

1.Alzheimer's Association
www.alz.org

2.Alzheimer's Foundation
www.alzfdn.org

3. Alzheimer's disease
www.ncbi.nlm.nih.gov

4.Alzheimer's disease - Wikipedia, the free encyclopedia
en.wikipedia.org/wiki/Alzheimer's_disease

5.Alzheimer's disease - MayoClinic.com
www.mayoclinic.com/health/alzheimers

6. Alzheimer's Basics - Alzheimer's Center - EverydayHealth.com
www.everydayhealth.com/senior-health/alzheimers

7. Understanding Dementia: Signs, Symptoms, Types, Causes, and Treatment

www.helpguide.org/elder/alzheimers_dementias_types

8. Dementia - WebMD: Types, Stages, Causes, Symptoms, Treatments
www.webmd.com


9. Lewy Body Dementia Association
www.lbda.org


10. Lewy body dementia - MayoClinic.com
www.mayoclinic.com/health/lewy-body-dementia


11. Dementia with Lewy bodies - Wikipedia, the free encyclopedia
en.wikipedia.org/wiki/Dementia_with_Lewy_bodies


12. Pick's disease (Frontotemporal dementia)
www.ncbi.nlm.nih.gov


13. Frontotemporal dementia - Wikipedia, the free encyclopedia
en.wikipedia.org/wiki/Frontotemporal_dementia


14. FCA: Frontotemporal Dementia
www.caregiver.org


15. FTD Caregiver Support Center - Home Page
www.ftdsupport.com


16. Alzheimer's Association - Frontotemporal Dementia
www.alz.org › Alzheimer's Disease › Related Dementias


17. Vascular Dementia: Signs, Symptoms, Prevention, and Treatment
www.helpguide.org/elder/vascular_dementia


18. Vascular Dementia
www.memorylossonline.com


19. National Stroke Association: Vascular Dementia Page
www.stroke.org


20. Multi-infarct dementia - Wikipedia, the free encyclopedia
en.wikipedia.org/wiki/Multi-infarct_dementia

21. Multi-infarct dementia
www.netdoctor.co.uk


22. Multi-Infarct Dementia Symptoms, Diagnosis, Treatments and Causes ...
www.wrongdiagnosis.com


23. Korsakoff's syndrome - Wikipedia, the free encyclopedia
en.wikipedia.org/wiki/Korsakoff's_syndrome


24. Wernicke-Korsakoff syndrome - causes, DSM, functioning, effects ...
www.minddisorders.com


25. Wernicke-Korsakoff Syndrome
www.webmd.com/brain/wernicke-korsakoff-syndrome


Caregiver Resources:


1. Help for Family Caregiver | caregiver.org
www.caregiver.org


2. Caregiving Resources - National Family Caregivers Association
www.nfcacares.org/caregiving_resources


3. Caregiver Resource Network
www.caregiverresource.ne


4. NATIONAL CAREGIVERS LIBRARY
www.caregiverslibrary.org


5. The Caregiver Resource Center, resources, financial, legal ...
www.caregiverresourcecenter.com


6. Regional Resources - Caregiver.com
www.caregiver.com/regionalresources

7. Are you caring for a - parent, spouse or someone else?
www.caringinfo.org


Free info and tips


8. Aging Parents | Elder Care | Senior Care
www.aging-parents-and-elder-care.com


9. Dementia Caregiver Resources, Inc.
www.dcrinc.org


10. National Alliance for Caregiving
www.caregiving.org


11. The Caregiver's Home Companion, elderly caregiving.
www.caregivershome.com


12. The Rosalynn Carter Institute for Caregiving - Caregiver Resources
www.rosalynncarter.org/caregiver_resources


13. National Family Caregivers Association
www.nfcacares.org


14. VA Caregivers Home
www.caregiver.va.gov


15. DCoE - VA Opens Toll-Free Caregiver Support Line
www.dcoe.health.mil


16. VA Caregiver Support Expanding | Dementia & Alzheimer's Weekly
www.alzheimersweekly.com


Telephone Help:


1. National VA/Caregiver Support Line- Toll free: 1-855-260-3274
2. Eldercare Locator: 1-800-677-1116

3. Alzheimer's Association:  1-(800) 272-3900


Medication Information:


These sites offer full information on medications and their side effects, many of which will not already be listed by the manufacturers. Remember, if you see a big change in your person after starting a new medication, you MUST gert them to the doctor ASAP.


1. Side Effects Of Medications
www.everydayhealth.com


2. Drug Side Effects
www.drugs.com


3. Drug Information: User Reviews ...
www.rxlist.com


4. WebMD  Medical information on prescription
www.webmd.com/drugs

5. Drugs
www.fda.gov


6. Pain Medications - Information About Pain Medicine
www.emedicinehealth.com


7. Drug Information, Side Effects & Interactions
www.drugwatch.com


8. Safe Medication
www.safemedication.com


9. The People's Pharmacy®
www.peoplespharmacy.com


10. Andrew Weil MD, famed for blended medicine guidance
DrWeil.com

Made in the USA
Lexington, KY
25 October 2013